Cloud Native Integration with Apache Camel

Building Agile and Scalable Integrations for Kubernetes Platforms

Guilherme Camposo

Apress®

Cloud Native Integration with Apache Camel: Building Agile and Scalable Integrations for Kubernetes Platforms

Guilherme Camposo
Rio De Janeiro, Brazil

ISBN-13 (pbk): 978-1-4842-7210-7   ISBN-13 (electronic): 978-1-4842-7211-4
https://doi.org/10.1007/978-1-4842-7211-4

Managing Director, Apress Media LLC: Welmoed Spahr
Acquisitions Editor: Divya Modi
Development Editor: Laura Berendson
Coordinating Editor: Divya Modi

Cover designed by eStudioCalamar

Cover image designed by Pixabay

Distributed to the book trade worldwide by Springer Science+Business Media New York, 1 New York Plaza, Suite 4600, New York, NY 10004-1562, USA. Phone 1-800-SPRINGER, fax (201) 348-4505, e-mail orders-ny@springer-sbm.com, or visit www.springeronline.com. Apress Media, LLC is a California LLC and the sole member (owner) is Springer Science + Business Media Finance Inc (SSBM Finance Inc). SSBM Finance Inc is a **Delaware** corporation.

For information on translations, please e-mail booktranslations@springernature.com; for reprint, paperback, or audio rights, please e-mail bookpermissions@springernature.com.

Apress titles may be purchased in bulk for academic, corporate, or promotional use. eBook versions and licenses are also available for most titles. For more information, reference our Print and eBook Bulk Sales web page at www.apress.com/bulk-sales.

Any source code or other supplementary material referenced by the author in this book is available to readers on GitHub via the book's product page, located at www.apress.com/978-1-4842-7210-7. For more detailed information, please visit www.apress.com/source-code.

Printed on acid-free paper

I dedicate this work to my beloved wife, who supports me in every moment of my life. I also would like to dedicate this work to my deceased grandmother and grandfather, who always believed in me and encouraged me to follow my dreams. I really wish you were here to share this moment with me.

Table of Contents

About the Author

Guilherme Camposo is a solution architect. He started using open-source projects early in his career and completely fell in love with the Open Source philosophy and potential, leading him to work with an open source company in 2018. Throughout his more than 12-year career, starting as a Java developer, becoming a consultant, and then an architect, Guilherme has acquired vast experience in helping customers from a great variety of business sectors, giving him a broad view on how integration and good software practices can help businesses to grow.

About the Technical Reviewer

 **Rodrigo Ramalho** is the Integration Leader for Latin America in the open-source company Red Hat.

In this role, he is responsible for spreading Red Hat's message of agile integration, leading customers on the API adoption journey through modern event-based architectures, microservices, and API management in multi-cloud container-based environments. He is an open-source enthusiast since a teenager and graduated in Computer Science in 2011. Also, he is a husband and father who likes to practice skydiving and surfing, and he is a brown belt in Brazilian Jiu-Jitsu.

Acknowledgments

I've always thought I should write a book. In my current profession, I often have to teach or explain a variety of technologies. I've also taught Java classes in the past but I never really tried to prepare myself to write a book. For that I would like to thank Divya Modi and Apress Media LLC for reaching out and giving me the amazing opportunity to write this book. I also would like to thank my friend Rodrigo Ramalho for doing a great job on this book's technical review, and all my colleagues and clients who influence me every day to keep studying and sharing knowledge.

Introduction

Building integration is a challenging task done by system architects and developers. Besides the complexity of intermediating the communication of at least two different systems, there is the necessity of adding complementary tools into the mix, like databases, message brokers, and access control tools, plus having to handle the integration tool itself. I want to support you in this challenge.

In *Cloud Native Integration With Apache Camel*, you will learn how to use an integration tool named Apache Camel. You'll learn how to integrate it with a database, a message broker, and how to deal with access control. We'll also discuss architecture and integration practices.

In the first chapter, you will learn the basis for your cloud native integration journey: how to build integration routes with Apache Camel and Quarkus. You will also understand the reason behind some decisions made for this approach to integration.

Chapter 2 is about the most popular cross-application communication architecture: REST APIs. You will see how to expose a route using REST and how to declare OAS definitions.

Chapter 3 describes how to secure and consume REST APIs using an open standard protocol, in this case OpenID Connect. You will learn a little bit about Keycloak, an identity and access management solution, and use it to work on access control.

In Chapter 4, I will show you how to access relational databases using Camel and Quarkus. You will also see how to work with transactions and how to properly handle exceptions in your integration routes.

Chapter 5 is related to asynchronous communication using message brokers. For the examples, you will use Apache Kafka, a very popular open-source message broker streaming platform. Good practices on declaring routes and approaches in unit tests will also be explored.

The last chapter focuses on how to deploy your integration application to Kubernetes and the good practices you must be aware of before putting the application into production. You will see how easy it is to test locally and how using Quarkus will make your development process really fast.

There are a bunch of patterns, architectures, and technologies to explore in this book. The knowledge you will gain will enable you to face the most common challenges in integration, so you will know everything you need to get started. I hope you enjoy this content as much as I enjoyed writing it. See you in Chapter 1.

CHAPTER 1

Welcome to Apache Camel

Systems integration is one of the most interesting challenges I face in my job as a solution architect, so it is definitely something I'm passionate about discussing and writing. I feel that most books are just too technical, covering everything that a specific tool does, or are just to theoretical, having great discussions about patterns and standards but not showing you how to solve problems with any tool. My problem with these two approaches is that sometimes you read a book, learn a new tool but do not understand how to apply it to different uses cases, or you know the theory too well but not how to apply it in the real world. Although there is plenty of space for these kinds of reading, such as when you want a technical manual for reference or you just want to expand your knowledge on a subject, my objective is to create a material that goes from an introductory perspective to a real-world, hands-on experience. I want you to get to know Apache Camel well, to develop a deeper understanding of integration practices, and to learn other complementary tools that you can use in different use cases. Most importantly, I want you to feel confident in your choices as an architect or as a developer.

There is a lot going on in this book. The idea is to have a real-world approach where you deal with a lot of different technologies, as you normally do in the field. I'm assuming you know a little bit of Java, Maven, containers, and Kubernetes, but don't worry if you do not feel like an

© Guilherme Camposo 2021
G. Camposo, *Cloud Native Integration with Apache Camel*,
https://doi.org/10.1007/978-1-4842-7211-4_1

expert on these technologies. I will approach them in a way that will make sense to everyone, from Java beginners who need to deploy applications to Kubernetes, to people who already have a solid knowledge of Java but maybe don't know Camel or need to learn an approach to develop in Java for containers.

In this first chapter, I will set the basis for everything you are going to do in this book. You will learn the basic concepts of the selected tools and, as you progress, we'll discuss the patterns and standards behind them. We are going from theoretical content to running applications.

The three main topics of this chapter are system integration, Apache Camel, and Java applications with Quarkus. Let's get started!

What Is System Integration?

Although the name is very self-explanatory, I want to be very clear on what I mean by system integration. Let's see some examples and discuss aspects related to this concept.

First, let's take the following scenario as an example:

> *Company A has bought an ERP (enterprise resource planning) system that, besides many other things, is responsible for the company's financial records. This company also acquired a system that, based on financial information, can create complete and graphical reports on the company's financial status, how efficient their investments are, how their products are selling, and so on. The problem is that the ERP system does not have a native way to input its information in the BI (business intelligence) system, and the BI system does not have a native way to consume information from the ERP system.*

The scenario above is a very common situation where two proprietary software programs need to "talk" to each other, but they are not built for this particular integration. This is what I meant when I said "native way", which means something already developed in the product. We need to create an integration layer between these two systems in order to make this work. Luckily for us, both systems are web API-oriented (application programming interface), allowing us to extract and input data using REST APIs. This way we can create an integration layer that can consume information from the ERP system, transform its data in a format accepted by the BI system, and then send this information to the BI system. You can see this illustrated in Figure 1-1.

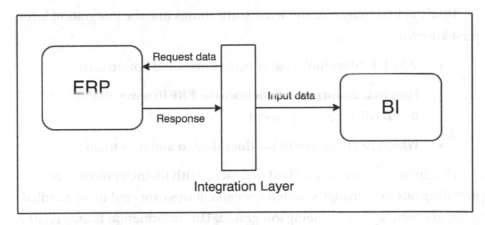

Figure 1-1. Integration layer between two systems

Despite being a very simple example, where I don't show you how this layer is built, it illustrates very well what this book means when I talk about system integration. In this sense, system integration is not just one application accessing another application. It is a system layer that can be composed of many applications, between two or more applications whose sole purpose is to integrate systems, not being directly responsible for business logic.

Let's see what separates those concepts.

Business or Integration Logic?

Business logic and integration logic are two different concepts. Although it may not be clear how to separate them, it is of great importance to know how to do so. Nobody wants to rewrite applications or integrations because you created a coupling situation, am I right? Let's define them and analyze some examples.

I finished the last section by saying that the integration layer shouldn't contain business logic, but "what does that mean?". Well, let me elaborate.

Take our first example. There are some things that the integration layer must know, like

- Which ERP endpoints to consume from and how to do it

- How to transform the data from the ERP in a way that the BI will be able to accept

- Which BI endpoints to produce data to and how to do it

This information is not related to dealing with financial records or providing business insights, which are capabilities expected to be handled by the respective systems being integrated. This information is only related to making the integration between the two systems work. Let's call this *integration logic*. Let's see another example to clarify what I mean by integration logic:

> *Imagine that System A is responsible for identifying customers who are in debt with our imaginary company. This company has a separate communication service that sends email, text messages, or even calls customers when they are in debt, but if a customer is in debt for more than two months, the Legal Service must be notified.*

If we consider that this situation is handled by an integration layer, it may seem that we have business logic inside our integration layer. That is why this is a good example to show the differences between business logic and integration logic.

Although the result of the analysis of how long this customer is in debt will ultimately impact on a process or business decision, this logic is inserted here with the sole purpose of dictating how the integration between these three services will happen. We could call this *routing*, because what is being done is determining where to send this notification. Take a look at Figure 1-2.

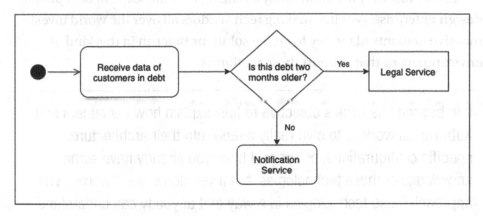

Figure 1-2. *Integration logic based on received data*

Removing the integration layer wouldn't mean that business information or data would get lost; it would only impact the integration of those services. If we had in this layer logic to determine how to calculate fees or how to negotiate this debt, it wouldn't be just an integration layer; it would be an actual service, where we would be inputting information from System A.

These are very short and simple examples just to get clear on what we are going to be approaching in this book. I will offer more complex and interesting cases to analyze as we go further. The idea is just to illustrate the concept, as I am going to do next for a cloud native application.

Cloud Native Applications

Now that I have clarified what I mean by saying *integration*, there is another term that you must know in order to fully understand this book's approach: *cloud native*.

One of the main objectives of this book is to give a modern approach on how to design and develop integrations, and at this point it's impossible to not talk about containers and Kubernetes. These technologies are so disruptive that they are completely changing the landscape of how people design enterprise systems, making tech vendors all over the world invest massive amounts of money to create solutions that run in this kind of environment or that support these platforms.

It is beyond this book's objective to fully explain how containers and Kubernetes work or to dive really deeply into their architectures, specific configurations, or usage. I hope you already have some knowledge of these technologies, but if you don't, don't worry. I will approach these technologies in a way that anybody can understand what we are doing and why we are doing it.

To set everyone on the same page, let's define these technologies.

Container: *"A way of packing and distributing applications and their dependencies, from libraries to runtimes. From an execution standpoint, it is also a way to isolate OS (operating system) processes, creating a sandbox for each container, similar to a virtual machine idea."*

A good way to understand containers is to compare them to a more commonly found technology, virtualization. Take a look at Figure 1-3.

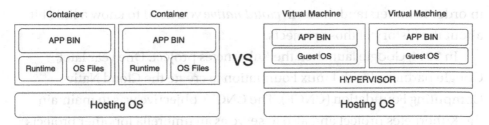

Figure 1-3. *Container representation*

Virtualization is a way to segregate physical machine resources to emulate a real machine. The Hypervisor is the software that manages the virtual machines and creates the hardware abstraction on top of one hosting operating system.

We virtualize for a number of different reasons: to isolate applications so they won't impact each other, to create different environments for applications that have different OS requirements or just different runtimes, to segregate physical resources per application, and so on. For some of these reasons, containerization may represent a much lighter way to achieve the same purpose, because it doesn't need a Hypervisor layer or hardware abstraction. It just reuses the hosting Linux kernel and allocates its resources per containers.

What about Kubernetes?

Kubernetes *"is an open source project focused on container orchestration at scale. It provides mechanisms and interfaces to allow container communication and management."*

Since we need software to manage a great number of virtual machines, or just to create high availability mechanisms, containers are no different. If we want to run containers at scale, we need complementary software to provide the required level of automation to do so. This is the importance of Kubernetes. It allows us to create clusters to manage and orchestrate containers at high scale.

This was a very high-level description of containers and Kubernetes. These descriptions give the idea of why we need these technologies, but in order to understand the term *cloud native* you need to know a little bit about the history of those projects.

In 2014, Google launched the Kubernetes project. One year later, Google partnered with Linux Foundation to create the Cloud Native Computing Foundation (CNCF). The CNCF's objective was to maintain the Kubernetes project and also to serve as an umbrella for other projects that Kubernetes is based on or that would compose the ecosystem. In this context, *cloud native* means "made for the Kubernetes ecosystem."

Besides the origin of CNCF, there are other reasons why the name "cloud" fits perfectly. Nowadays Kubernetes can be easily considered an industry standard. This is particularly true when thinking about the big public cloud providers (e.g. AWS, Azure and GCP). All of them have Kubernetes services or container-based solutions, and all of them are contributors to the Kubernetes project. The project is also present in the solutions of players providing private cloud solutions such as IBM, Oracle, or VMWare. Even niche players that create solutions for specific uses such as logging, monitoring, and NoSQL databases have their products ready for containers or are creating solutions specifically for containers and Kubernetes. This shows how important Kubernetes and containers have become.

For the most part of this book I will be focusing on integration cases and the technologies to solve those cases, but all the decisions made will take into consideration cloud native application best practices. After you have solid understanding of integration technologies and patterns, in the last chapter you will dive into how to deploy and configure developed applications in Kubernetes.

So let's talk about our main integration tool.

What is Apache Camel?

First and foremost, you must understand what Apache Camel is and what Apache Camel is not, before starting to code and dive in integration cases.

Apache Camel is a framework written in Java that allows developers to create integrations in an easy and standardized way, using concepts of well-established integration patterns. Camel has a super interesting structure called *components*, where each component encapsulates the logic necessary to access different endpoints, such as databases, message brokers, HTTP applications, file systems, and so on. It also has components for integration with specific services, such as Twitter, Azure, and AWS, totaling over 300 components, making it a perfect Swiss knife for integration.

There a few low-code/no-code solutions to create integration. Some of these tools are even written using Camel, such as the open-source project Syndesis. Here you are going to learn how to write integration with Java using Camel as an integration specialized framework.

Let's learn the basics.

Integration Logic, Integration Routing

You are going to start by analyzing the following "Hello World" example shown in Listing 1-1.

Listing 1-1. HelloWorldRoute.java File

```
package com.appress.integration;
import org.apache.camel.builder.RouteBuilder;
public class HelloWorldRoute extends RouteBuilder {
    @Override
    public void configure() throws Exception {
        from("timer:example?period=2000")
```

```
        .setBody(constant("Hello World"))
        .to("log:" + HelloWorldRoute.class.getName() );
    }
}
```

This class creates a timer application that prints Hello World in the console every 2 seconds. Although this is not a real integration case, it can help you understand Camel more easily, because is better to start small, one bite at a time.

There are just a few lines of code here, but there is a lot going on.

The first thing to notice is that the HelloWorldRoute class extends a Camel class called RouteBuilder. Every integration built with Camel uses a concept called a **route**. The idea is that an integration always starts from an endpoint and then goes to one or multiples endpoints. That is exactly what is happening with this Hello World example.

The **route** starts with a timer **component** (from) and eventually hits the final destination, which is the log **component** (to). Another thing worth mentioning is that you have a single line of code to create your route, although it is indented to make it more readable. This is because Camel utilizes a fluent way to write routes where you can append definitions on how your route should behave or simply set attributes to your route.

Route builders, such as the class HelloWorldRoute, are just blueprints. This means that this type of class is only executed when the application is starting. By executing the configure() method, the outcome of these stacked calls is a **route definition** and it is used to instantiated many objects in memory. These objects in memory will react to events being triggered to or by the from (consumer) endpoint. In this particular case, the component will auto-generate its events that will go through the route logic until it reaches its final endpoint. This execution of an incoming event is called an **Exchange**.

Exchanges and Messages

You saw in the last section how the integration logic is created and executed, but how will the data be handled in this step-by-step execution? Routes carry other structures in order to make the integration work. Let's see.

There was one line of code left to comment about in the last example. The setBody(constant("Hello World")) is the only line where you actually set data in your route. Let's see how data is handled within routes.

In the previous section, I said: *"Those objects in memory will react to events being triggered to or by the from() endpoint."*. In this case, when I'm talking about an event, I mean that the timer triggered, but it could be an incoming HTTP request, a file hitting a directory, or another triggered action from different endpoints. What is important is that when that happens, an object called Exchange is created. This object is the data representation of the route execution. This means that every time the timer triggers, a new Exchange will be created, and that object will be available until that execution is finished. Take a look at the Exchange representation on Figure 1-4.

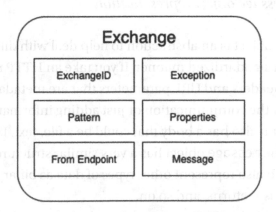

Figure 1-4. Exchange representation

11

The above representation shows the main attributes available in an Exchange object. All of them are important, but if you want to understand what setBody(constant("Hello World")) does, you must focus on the message.

Every endpoint you hit in your route chain has the potential to change the Exchange state, and most of the time they will do it by interacting with the Message attribute.

The message object represents the data coming and going, to and from the different endpoints within your route. Look at the representation of the message object in Figure 1-5.

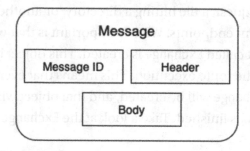

Figure 1-5. *Message object representation*

The message object is an abstraction to help deal with different types of data in a standardized manner. If you take an HTTP request, for example, it has headers and URL parameters that are metadata describing characteristics of the communication or just adding information in a key/value format, but it also has a body that could be a file, text, JSON, or many other formats. The message object has a very similar structure, but it is flexible enough to also represent other types of data as binary files, JMS messages, database returns, and so on.

Continuing with the HTTP request example, headers and URL parameters would be parsed to message header attributes and the HTTP body would became a message body.

When you did setBody(constant("Hello World")) you changed the message object in the exchange, by setting the string "Hello World" as the body attribute.

There is one thing left to explain. What does constant("Hello World") mean?

Expression Languages

The route class is just a blueprint, so it won't execute more than one time. So how do we deal with data dynamically? One possible answer is expression languages.

The setBody() method receives as an argument an object of the type **Expression**. This happens because this route step could be static or it could change depending on what data is going through the route, and that needs to be evaluated during the route creation. In this case, you want that every time a new event is triggered by the timer, the body message should be set to "Hello World". To do that, you used the method constant(). This method allows you to set a static value as a constant, in this case a string value, or to get a value at runtime and also use it as a constant. No matter what is being executed, the value will always be the same.

The constant() method is not the only way of dealing with the exchange data. There are other expression languages that fit different purposes. All available ELs in Camel are listed in Table 1-1.

Table 1-1. *Camel-Supported Expression Languages*

Bean Method	Constant	CSimple	DataSonnet	Exchange Property
Xquery	Xpath	XML Tokenize	Tokenize	SpEL
ExchangeProperty	File	Groovy	Header	HL7 Terser
jOOR	JsonPath	MVEL	OGNL	Ref
Simple				

You will see examples with other expression languages in the future.

Now that you have a complete understanding of how the `Hello World` example works, you need to run this code. But there is a missing piece. How do you pack and run this code? For that you need to understand Quarkus first.

Quarkus

You will use cloud native principles and you will distribute your applications as container images, but this is the last step in the process. How do you handle the application dependencies? How do you compile Java classes? How do you run Java code? To answer these questions, you need Quarkus.

You are almost getting to the point where you can run Camel applications. You have a basic understanding of how Camel works. Now you will tackle the base framework.

Quarkus is an open source project released in 2018. It was made especially for the Kubernetes world, creating a mechanism to make Java development for Kubernetes a lot easier, and also dealing with Java "old" problems.

To understand why Quarkus is important, you need to understand the Java "old" problems. Let's talk about history.

Java Evolution

Let's step back and understand how Java was used for enterprise applications before Quarkus came into place.

Java was first released in 1995, almost 26 years ago. It is safe to say that the world has changed a lot since then, let alone the IT industry.

The idea of having a virtual machine capable of executing bytecodes, giving developers the possibility of writing code that could run in any operating system, was brilliant. It created a huge community around the Java language, making it one of the most, or maybe *the* most, popular programming language. Another feature that made huge impact on its popularity was the capacity to self-manage memory allocation, freeing developers of dealing with pointers to allocate memory space. But everything good comes with a price. The JVM (Java Virtual Machine), which is the "native" program responsible for translating Java bytecodes to machine code, requires computer resources to exist and at that point in history it was ok to spent a few megabytes on a virtual machine structure.

The majority of the enterprise application written, and here I'm talking somewhere between 2000 and 2010, were deployed in an application server. Websphere, JBoss, and Web Logic were huge back then, and I dare to say they still are, but not as much as in their glory days. Application servers provided centralized capabilities such as security, resource sharing, configuration management, scalability, logging, and so on, with a very small price to pay: a few megabytes for the virtual machine and a few megabytes for the application server code itself, besides additional CPU usage. That price would be diluted if you could deploy a bunch of applications in the same server.

To make them highly available, a system administrator would create a cluster for that particular application server, deploying every application at least twice, once for each node of the cluster.

Even though you could achieve high availability, scalability wasn't necessarily easy, and definitely not cheap. You had the option to scale everything by adding another node identical to what you had in your cluster, which sometimes would scale applications that didn't need to be scaled, therefore spending resources without necessity. You also could create different profiles and different clusters for specific applications because there were application that couldn't be scaled and required a profile of their own. Here you could have ended in a situation where you need to have a single application per application server because the characteristics of the applications were too different from each other, making harder to plan their lifecycle together.

At this point, the price to pay to have an application server started to get higher and higher, even with AS vendors trying to make their platform as modular as possible to dodge those problems. Applications started to evolve in a different way to solve those situations.

Microservices

The cloud native way is often built on top of the *microservices architecture*. Here I will describe what it is and how it relates to the Java evolution, and most importantly, the Java framework ecosystem.

As you saw in the last section, to scale application servers wasn't an easy task. It took a specific strategy depending on your application and a lot of computational resources. Another problem was dealing with application library dependencies.

One of the things that makes the Java community so strong is how easy it is to distribute and obtain reusable libraries. Using tools like Gradle, Maven, or even Maven's older brother Ant, it was possible to pack your code into a jar/war/ear and incorporate the dependencies your application needed, or you could just deploy your dependencies straight to your application server and share them with every application on that server. This mechanism was used by numerous Java projects. Nothing was just created. Everything was reused when possible. That's fine, until you have to put different applications on the same application server.

In the begging of the application server era, handling dependency conflicts was chaotic. You could, and still can, have applications using the same library but different versions of it, and the versions may be completely incompatible. It was a true class-loading hell. Who back then didn't receive an NoSuchMethodError exception? Of course application servers have evolved to deal with these issues. They created isolation mechanisms so every application could have its own class loading process, or could specify exactly which dependencies it would use, using for example the OSGi framework, but this didn't solve the risk of putting all of the eggs in the same basket. If one application had, for example, a memory leak problem, it would affect every application running on the same JVM.

Around 2013~2014, multiple projects started to be released with the idea of creating independent runnable jar applications. Projects such as Spring Boot, Dropwizards and Thorntail developed frameworks that made development easier and faster. Adopting principles such as standardization-over-configuration, those framework would allow developers to create applications faster by coding less lines of code and still getting most of the benefits of the JAVA EE specification without relying on application servers. Your source code, your dependencies, and the framework itself would be packed in single, isolated, runnable jar file, also known as a fat jar. During the same years, REST became really popular.

Having a way to pack your application and a reliable protocol to provide inter-service communication allowed developers to adopt a more scalable and modular style of architecture: microservices.

The microservice conversation is a long one. To really define a microservice we could discuss service granularity, domain definitions, technology specialization, services lifecycle, and other aspects that could interfere with how we architect our applications, but to avoid deviating too much from our main topic, let's agree on the understanding that microservices are services designed to be more concise/specialized, spreading a system complexity throughout multiple services.

Now we are closer to 2018. The fat jar frameworks are the real deal, and with a small pinch of automation, they take the space occupied by application servers. This model translates well to containers, because we just need the jar and the runtime (JRE) to run it. It's easy to create a container image to pack your application and runtime dependencies. This was the easiest way to bring Java to containers and Kubernetes.

Now instead of deploying ten war files to an application server, these ten new services are packed into ten different container images, creating ten JVM process running as containers, which are orchestrated by your Kubernetes cluster.

It is easier and faster than ever to develop and deploy services written in Java, but the problem now is: how much resource are you spending here?

Do you remember when I said about the small price to have a Java Virtual Machine? Now this price is multiplied by ten. Do you remember when I talked about the extreme reuse of libraries and how chaotic it was in a shared environment? Well, now we don't have dependency conflicts because the services are isolated, but we still have a ton of dependencies in those frameworks, and we are replicating this. The fat jars are really getting fatter, making the class loading process slower and heavier, sometimes consuming more CPU in the startup time than when the application is really running. We are also consuming more memory. Having many microservices running in Java is now very resource expensive.

I wanted to go throughout this history so you can understand why we are going to use Quarkus for our integrations. Quarkus was created when all those problems were set. So it was created to solve them. Its libraries were coded from scratch, giving it a much faster class-loading process and a much smaller memory footprint. It was also designed for the Kubernetes world, so it's much easier to deploy it in containers and interact with Kubernetes environment. We could use Camel with another framework, but our focus is to build cloud native integrations. This is why I chose Quarkus.

Let's stop talking and let's start coding.

Development Requirements

A few tools will be necessary to run the code examples in this book. They will be the same tools used to run the examples in all chapters.

The source code for this book is available on GitHub via the book's product page, located at www.apress.com/ISBN. There you will find the first example code, called camel-hello-world, that we will be addressing now.

Here is the list of tools used:

- JDK 11 installed with JAVA_HOME configured appropriately

- Maven 3.6.3 with M2_HOME configured

- Quarkus 1.13.0.Final

- Camel 3.9.0

- Docker CE 20.10.5

- A terminal or prompt to run commands

Since instructions may vary between different operating systems, I won't cover how to install and configure Java, Maven, and Docker. You can find that information on each project's website.

This book is IDE agnostic. Use the IDE you are most comfortable with. You are going to need a terminal or prompt to run Maven and Docker commands, so have one properly set. The only plugins you will use are Maven plugins, which should be compatible with all major OSes.

Let's start by downloading the book's code. After you are done, go to the project camel-hello-world directory. It should look like Figure 1-6.

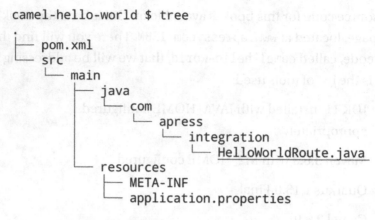

```
camel-hello-world $ tree
.
├── pom.xml
└── src
    └── main
        ├── java
        │   └── com
        │       └── apress
        │           └── integration
        │               └── HelloWorldRoute.java
        └── resources
            ├── META-INF
            └── application.properties

8 directories, 3 files
```

Figure 1-6. *Quarkus directory structure*

As you can see in Figure 1-6, there are only three files in this Maven project: the route class you already know, the `application.properties` file, and the `pom.xml` file.

It is beyond the scope of this book to teach Maven. I hope you already have some familiarity with the tool, but if you don't, don't worry. I will give you all the commands needed and you will use the pom files provided with the source code. You just need to have Maven configured in your machine. For information on how to install and configure Maven, go to `https://maven.apache.org/`.

Let's take a look at the snippet in Listing 1-2 from the `pom.xml` file.

Listing 1-2. Camel-hello-world pom.xml Snippet

```
...
  <dependencyManagement>
    <dependencies>
      <dependency>
        <groupId>io.quarkus</groupId>
        <artifactId>quarkus-universe-bom</artifactId>
        <version>1.13.0.Final</version>
        <type>pom</type>
        <scope>import</scope>
      </dependency>
    </dependencies>
  </dependencyManagement>
...
```

This is a very important part of the pom. This section describes
the reference from where you are going to retrieve the versions of all
dependencies used in this book. Quarkus provides a "bill of materials"
dependency called quarkus-universe-bom, where every component of
the framework is declared. This way you won't need to worry about every
dependency version and the compatibility between them.

Listing 1-3 shows the project dependencies.

Listing 1-3. Camel-hello-world pom.xml snippet

```
...
  <dependencies>
    <dependency>
      <groupId>org.apache.camel.quarkus</groupId>
      <artifactId>camel-quarkus-log</artifactId>
    </dependency>
    <dependency>
```

```
        <groupId>org.apache.camel.quarkus</groupId>
        <artifactId>camel-quarkus-core</artifactId>
    </dependency>
    <dependency>
        <groupId>org.apache.camel.quarkus</groupId>
        <artifactId>camel-quarkus-timer</artifactId>
    </dependency>
  </dependencies>
...
```

The dependencies present in the Quarkus bill of materials are called *extensions*. In the first example, there are only three, which is great. This way the code will be simpler and lighter. This is possible because, besides being a brand new framework, Quarkus implements the MicroProfile specification. Let's talk a little bit about it.

The MicroProfile Specification

Technologies always evolve, and sometimes they become so important for an ecosystem that we may need a specification for them. This helps the ecosystem to grow because it offers more interoperability between different projects. The MicroProfile specification is one of those cases.

This has happened in the past. We can use Hibernate as an example. It became so popular and important for the Java community that this ORM (object-relational mapping) project drove many aspects of what would become the JPA (Java Persistence API) specification, which affected the Java language itself.

History was repeated with the MicroProfile specification and the microservices frameworks (Spring Boot, Quarkus, Thorntail, and so on). As they grew in popularity, and more and more projects provided new functionalities to this ecosystem, a specification was required to guarantee minimum interoperability between them and also to set requirements and good practices for these frameworks.

The MicroProfile specification is the equivalent of the Jakarta EE (formerly known as Java Platform, Enterprise Edition – Java EE) for the microservices frameworks. It translates a subset of the (Application Programming Interfaces) API's specifications present in the Jakarta EE to the microservice universe. It's only a subset because there are components that do not make sense for this different approach and the main concern here is to be micro and yet effective.

Here is a list of the APIs present in the specification:

- Logging

- Configuration

- Fault Tolerance

- Health Check

- Metrics

- Open API

- Rest API

- JWT Authentication

- OpenTracing

- Dependency Injection (CDI)

- JSON-P (Parsing)

- JSON-B (Binding)

Although the majority of these APIs are required for every microservice, each one is independent. This modularity helps us to maintain our services as thin as possible, since we only import the dependencies that we are going to use.

MicroProfile is currently in version 4.0.

By choosing Quarkus as our base framework for Camel, we are also getting access to the MicroProfile specification power. So let's get back to our code.

Running the Code

Now that you have information about how the tools work and how they came to be, let's start running the example code.

There is one more thing worth mention about the pom.xml file: the quarkus-maven-plugin. Take a look at Listing 1-4.

Listing 1-4. Camel-hello-world pom.xml Snippet

```
...
    <plugin>
        <groupId>io.quarkus</groupId>
        <artifactId>quarkus-maven-plugin</artifactId>
        <version>1.13.0.Final</version>
        <extensions>true</extensions>
        <executions>
          <execution>
            <goals>
              <goal>build</goal>
              <goal>generate-code</goal>
              <goal>generate-code-tests</goal>
            </goals>
          </execution>
        </executions>
    </plugin>
...
```

This plugin is extremely important for Quarkus. It is responsible for building, packing, and debugging the code.

In order to achieve faster startup times, the Quarkus plugin does a little bit more than just compilation. It anticipates tasks that the majority of the frameworks do in runtime, like loading libraries and configuration files, scanning the application's classpath, configuring the dependency injection, setting up object-relational mapping, instantiating REST controllers, and so on. This strategy mitigates two undesirable behaviors for cloud native applications:

- Applications taking longer to be ready to receive requests or start

- Applications consuming more CPU and memory in the startup than when actually running

You can't run your code without this plugin, so remember to have it configured when creating your Quarkus applications. Let's run the camel-hello-world code.

In your terminal, go to the camel-hello-world directory and run the following command:

```
camel-hello-world $ mvn quarkus:dev
```

If it is the first time you are running Quarkus applications in this version, it may take a few minutes to download all of the dependencies. After that, you will see the application log as shown in Listing 1-5.

Listing 1-5. Application Output

```
__  ____  __  _____   ___  __ ____  _____ 
 --/ __ \/ / / / _ | / _ \/ //_/ / / / __/ 
 -/ /_/ / /_/ / __ |/ , _/ ,< / /_/ /\ \   
--_____/_/ |_/_/|_/_/|_|\____/___/   
2021-04-04 19:43:20,118 INFO  [org.apa.cam.qua.cor.
CamelBootstrapRecorder] (main) bootstrap runtime: org.apache.
camel.quarkus.main.CamelMainRuntime
2021-04-04 19:43:20,363 INFO  [org.apa.cam.imp.eng.
AbstractCamelContext] (main) Routes startup summary (total:1
started:1)
```

```
2021-04-04 19:43:20,363 INFO  [org.apa.cam.imp.eng.
AbstractCamelContext] (main)      Started route1 (timer://example)
2021-04-04 19:43:20,363 INFO  [org.apa.cam.imp.eng.
AbstractCamelContext] (main) Apache Camel 3.9.0 (camel-1)
started in 86ms (build:0ms init:68ms start:18ms)
2021-04-04 19:43:20,368 INFO  [io.quarkus] (main) camel-hello-
world 1.0.0 on JVM (powered by Quarkus 1.13.0.Final) started in
1.165s.
2021-04-04 19:43:20,369 INFO  [io.quarkus] (main) Profile prod
activated.
2021-04-04 19:43:20,370 INFO  [io.quarkus] (main) Installed
features: [camel-core, camel-log, camel-support-common, camel-
timer, cdi]
2021-04-04 19:43:21,369 INFO  [com.app.int.HelloWorldRoute]
(Camel (camel-1) thread #0 - timer://example) Exchange
[ExchangePattern: InOnly, BodyType: String, Body: Hello World]
2021-04-04 19:43:23,367 INFO  [com.app.int.HelloWorldRoute] (Camel
(camel-1) thread #0 - timer://example) Exchange[ExchangePattern:
InOnly, BodyType: String, Body: Hello World]
2021-04-04 19:43:25,370 INFO  [com.app.int.HelloWorldRoute]
(Camel (camel-1) thread #0 - timer://example)
Exchange[ExchangePattern: InOnly, BodyType: String, Body: Hello
World]
```

This is your first interaction with the plugin, by calling quarkus:dev. Here you are using Quarkus development mode. This mode will run your application locally and allow you to test it. It also allows you to remote debug your code. By default it will listen for debuggers on port 5005.

Alright, so you were finally able to run some code, but how do you pack the application for distribution? Let's see next.

Packing Applications

To run a Java application you need at least a jar file. How do you provide that with Quarkus?

The integration code is packed using Quarkus, a cloud native microservice framework, and as such, you know you are going to run it in a container, but before you can create your container image, you need to understand how to create an executable file. In Quarkus, there are two ways of doing it: traditional JVM or native compilation.

We have been discussing JVM, class loading, and how Quarkus optimizes the process by anticipating some runtime steps in the build process, but there is a method to go even further in trying to optimize application performance: the native compilation.

Native Image is one running mode of **GraalVM**, a JDK project developed by Oracle to improve the code execution of Java and other JVM languages. In this mode, a native executable is created by the compiler. By native, I mean "code that doesn't required a JVM and runs natively for each operating system it has been compiled to." The resulting executable has a much faster startup time and a smaller memory footprint. This is highly desirable if I'm running hundreds of services.

This happens because the code is precompiled and some classes are initialized in advance. So there is no need for bytecode interpretation. Some JVM functionalities, such as the garbage collector, which is a way to deal with memory allocation, are built in the resulting binary. This way you don't lose much by not having a JVM.

As you can imagine, there are some points of attention to be able to use this method of compilation. Things like reflection, dynamic class loading, and serialization work differently in the native approach because of the ahead-of-time compilation, making some commonly used Java libraries incompatible.

Quarkus is born for this new world and it is GraalVM compatible, but in this book we will focus on the traditional JVM bytecode compilation.

My idea is to maintain focus on integration and Camel, but every pom.
xml in this book's examples will have the native profile configured, so you
can try native compilation when you feel like it. Just remember that there
is a lot of processing during native compilation, making the compilation
process a little longer and consuming a lot more memory and CPU.

Well, now that you know of the existence of native compilation and
GraalVM, let's go back to the runnable jar approach. Quarkus offers two
ways of packing jars: fast jar or uber jar.

Fast Jar

Fast jar is a different way to create runnable jars. It is the default packing
option of Quarkus 1.13. You are going to see next how it works.

Open a terminal and run the following command under the camel-
hello-world folder to start packing the application:

```
camel-hello-world $ mvn package
```

This will generate one folder called target, where Maven leaves
the build resulting files. Look at the directory structure; it should be like
Figure 1-7.

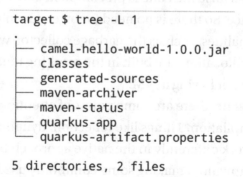

```
target $ tree -L 1
.
├── camel-hello-world-1.0.0.jar
├── classes
├── generated-sources
├── maven-archiver
├── maven-status
├── quarkus-app
└── quarkus-artifact.properties

5 directories, 2 files
```

Figure 1-7. *Maven's target generated folder*

Go to the quarkus-app folder and list its contents, as in Figure 1-8

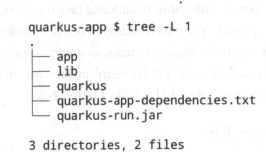

```
quarkus-app $ tree -L 1
.
├── app
├── lib
├── quarkus
├── quarkus-app-dependencies.txt
└── quarkus-run.jar

3 directories, 2 files
```

Figure 1-8. *quarkus-app folder structure*

As you can see, the structure here is a little bit different than what you usually get when trying to pack runnable jars using Maven. Although you have a jar file in the target folder, the camel-hello-world-1.0.0.jar does not contain the required MANIFEST.MF information for this jar to be runnable. It only contains the compiled code and resource files. Quarkus-maven-plugin will generate the quarkus-app folder where the structure will be used to run the application.

Let's try it out. Run the following command under the /camel-hello-world/target/quarkus-app folder:

```
quarkus-app $ java -jar quarkus-run.jar
```

After this the Hello World application should start running. Look for a log entry like the following:

```
2021-04-10 15:13:10,314 INFO [org.apa.cam.imp.eng.
AbstractCamelContext] (main) Apache Camel 3.9.0 (camel-1)
started in 88ms (build:0ms init:63ms start:25ms)
```

This log entry shows how long it took to start the application. In my case, it was 88 milliseconds, which is pretty fast. Your result will probably be different than mine, because this depends on the machine's overall performance. Disk, CPU, and RAM speeds will influence the speed of your machine. You may have a faster or slower result, but you can see that Quarkus is fast compared with more traditional Java frameworks.

In the fast jar approach, the class loading process is broken down to boot dependencies and main dependencies, as you can see by examining the files. Unzip the quarkus-run.jar (remember, jars are zip files) and take a look at the manifest file. It should look like Listing 1-6.

Listing 1-6. Manifest File

```
Manifest-Version: 1.0
Class-Path:  lib/boot/org.jboss.logging.jboss-logging--
3.4.1.Final.jar li b/boot/org.jboss.logmanager.jboss-
logmanager-embedded-1.0.9.jar lib/boo t/org.graalvm.sdk.
graal-sdk-21.0.0.jar lib/boot/org.wildfly.common.wild fly-
common-1.5.4.Final-format-001.jar lib/boot/io.smallrye.common.
small rye-common-io-1.5.0.jar lib/boot/io.quarkus.quarkus-
bootstrap-runner-1. 13.0.Final.jar lib/boot/io.quarkus.quarkus-
development-mode-spi-1.13.0.
 Final.jar
Main-Class: io.quarkus.bootstrap.runner.QuarkusEntryPoint
Implementation-Title: camel-hello-world
Implementation-Version: 1.0.0
```

As you can see, there are no classes in this jar. The class-path points to Quarkus' dependencies only and the main-class attribute points to a Quarkus class. The code will be packed in the quarkus-app/app directory and the dependencies you use to work with Camel will be in the quarkus-app/lib/main directory. This process guarantees that the foundational classes are loaded first, in this case Quarkus classes, and then your code will be loaded, making the startup process smarter and, therefore, faster.

Let's see the other approach.

Uber Jar

This is a more traditional packing style commonly found in other microservices-oriented frameworks. Let's see how to use it.

Uber jars, or fat jars, are a very simple concept: put everything you need, from a source code standpoint, in a single place and just run this jar. Having everything in a single file makes things easier, like distributing the application, although it can create large files sometimes. Since fast jar is the default option, you need to tell quarkus-maven-plugin that you want to override the default behavior. There are different ways of telling the plugin how you want your packing style to be. Let's see the first one.

Run the following command in the camel-hello-world folder:

```
camel-hello-world $ mvn clean package \
-Dquarkus.package.type=uber-jar
```

By passing the quarkus.package.type parameter with value uber-jar, the plugin will modify its behavior and create an uber-jar.

Both the Quarkus framework and quarkus-maven-plugin react to configurations passed as environment variables, JVM properties, or configurations present in the application.properties file. You will learn more about this in a future chapter.

Check the uber-jar created in the camel-hello-world/target/ folder as illustrated by Figure 1-9.

```
target $ tree -L 1
.
├── camel-hello-world-1.0.0-runner.jar
├── camel-hello-world-1.0.0.jar.original
├── classes
├── generated-sources
├── maven-archiver
├── maven-status
└── quarkus-artifact.properties

4 directories, 3 files
```

Figure 1-9. *Uber-jar build result*

To run the application, execute the following command in the `camel-hello-world/target/` folder:

```
target $ java -jar camel-hello-world-1.0.0-runner.jar
```

After the application starts running, wait a few seconds and stop it. Find the log entry to identify how long it took to start the application. Here is my result:

```
2021-04-10 17:37:36,875 INFO  [org.apa.cam.imp.eng.
AbstractCamelContext] (main) Apache Camel 3.9.0 (camel-1)
started in 115ms (build:0ms init:89ms start:26ms)
```

As you can see, it took 115ms to start the application in my computer, which is still a very nice startup time. When compared to the results from the fast jar building, which was 88ms, the difference is 27ms. It may not seem much in absolute value, but it represents an increase of approximately 32% in startup time.

Well, now you have the understanding of how to pack Java code using `quarkus-maven-plugin`. This is going to help you to distribute your code, especially in standalone applications, that you can configure as a service in the OS. You may ask, what about containers and Kubernetes? Let's see next.

Container Images

One important step to achieve the cloud native status is to be able to run in a container, and in order to run in a container, you need a container image first. Let's see how Quarkus can help with this task.

You are almost done with the important task of packing your application for distribution and installation. Since you are targeting a cloud native approach, you need to know how to create an OCI (Open Container Initiative) compliant image. By the way, I didn't talk about the OCI organization with you before. I think now is a good time.

Established in June 2015, the OCI is a Linux Foundation project, as is the CNCF, which was designed to create open industry standards around container formats and runtimes. So when I said "we need to know how to create an OCI compliant image", I'm looking for a way to distribute my application as a container image that can run in multiple runtimes that are also OCI compliant.

Having said that, it's time to create your first image using Quarkus.

The first thing you need to do is add a new Quarkus extension to your Maven project. To do so, run the following command under the camel-hello-world folder as follows:

```
camel-hello-world $ mvn quarkus:add-extension \
-Dextensions="container-image-jib"
```

This is a new trick for you. With the plugin goal quarkus:add-extension you can manipulate your pom structure in a simplified way. This command will add the dependencies you need using the version you have mapped in the Quarkus bill of materials, so you don't need to worry about compatibility.

Quarkus has a pretty extensive list of extensions. You can search for them using the same plugin. Run this command:

```
camel-hello-world $ mvn quarkus:list-extensions
```

You will get a list of the extensions present in the particular bom version you are using. You can also get more detailed information by running the command like this:

```
camel-hello-world $ mvn quarkus:list-extensions \
-Dquarkus.extension.format=full
```

This will show you the extensions available and point out the extension documentation. You can use this command to find out more about the extension you are using, container-image-jib, such as how to change the tag, name, or registry in the generated image. For now, you are going to set only the group name to have consistency because this configuration, by default, will use the OS running user username. This way I can show a command that everyone can use without adaptation.

Going back to the original purpose, which is to generate a container image, you already have the extension set. Let's pack the application. Run this command:

```
camel-hello-world $ mvn clean package \
-Dquarkus.container-image.build=true \
-Dquarkus.container-image.group=localhost
```

You may see that part of the Maven's build is creating a container image. It should look like Listing 1-7.

Listing 1-7.   Maven Output

```
[INFO] --- quarkus-maven-plugin:1.13.0.Final:build (default) @
camel-hello-world ---
[INFO] [org.jboss.threads] JBoss Threads version 3.2.0.Final
[INFO] [io.quarkus.container.image.jib.deployment.JibProcessor]
Starting container image build
[WARNING] [io.quarkus.container.image.jib.deployment.
JibProcessor] Base image 'fabric8/java-alpine-openjdk11-
```

jre' does not use a specific image digest - build may not be reproducible

```
[INFO] [io.quarkus.container.image.jib.deployment.JibProcessor]
The base image requires auth. Trying again for fabric8/java-
alpine-openjdk11-jre...
[INFO] [io.quarkus.container.image.jib.deployment.JibProcessor]
Using base image with digest: sha256:b459cc59d6c7ddc9fd52f981fc
4c187f44a401f2433a1b4110810d2dd9e98a07
[INFO] [io.quarkus.container.image.jib.deployment.JibProcessor]
Container entrypoint set to [java, -Djava.util.logging.
manager=org.jboss.logmanager.LogManager, -jar, quarkus-run.jar]
[INFO] [io.quarkus.container.image.jib.deployment.JibProcessor]
Created container image localhost/camel-hello-world:1.0.0 (sh
a256:fe4697492c2e9a19030e6e557832e8a75b5459be08cd86a0cf9a636a
cd225871)
```

The extension is using 'fabric8/java-alpine-openjdk11-jre' as your base image (the image that you will create your image upon). This image will provide the OS files and the runtime you need, in this case JDK 11. The created image uses localhost as the image group name, the Maven artifact id (camel-hello-world) as the image name, and the Maven project version (1.0.0) as the image tag. The resulting image will be saved to your local image registry. You can check that out by running

```
$ docker image ls
```

You should see something like Figure 1-10.

```
~ $ docker image ls
REPOSITORY                    TAG      IMAGE ID       CREATED         SIZE
localhost/camel-hello-world   1.0.0    d49f4e6e607c   3 minutes ago   212MB
```

Figure 1-10. *Resulting container image*

To check if everything is configured as planned, let's run the generated container image:

```
$ docker run -it --name hello-world localhost/camel-hello-world:1.0.0
```

You're using the options -it (-i is for interactive and -t is for a pseudo terminal) so you can see the application logs as you do when running it locally and you can stop it by using Control + c. You set a container name, using --name, to make it easier to identify the container in the future.

Let's check this image from inside. Open a new terminal/prompt window and get the hello-world container running. Execute the following command to open a terminal inside your container:

```
$ docker exec -it hello-world sh
```

A terminal will open and you will be directed to the container workspace. Check its content by listing the directory as in Figure 1-11.

```
~ $ docker exec -it hello-world sh
/work # ls
app              lib              quarkus         quarkus-run.jar
```

Figure 1-11. *Container content*

As you can see, the resulting image is using the fast jar approach. This way you can take advantage of this method being faster and you didn't need to worry about how to pack it or how to configure the image, because the plugin did everything for you.

Summary

In this chapter, I set the basis for everything we are going to do in this book. You learned about the following:

- What system integration is and how you are going to approach it

- Cloud native applications and the history-related projects and organizations behind them

- An introduction to Apache Camel, what it is, and its basic concepts

- The Java language evolution

- Patterns and specifications that set the standards you will follow in your implementations

- What you need to know about Quarkus to be able to deliver Camel applications for integration

Now that you have basic knowledge of Camel, and you know how to pack and run your integrations, you will learn more about Camel and how to resolve integration challenges, as we discuss patterns and standards along the way.

In the next chapter, you start addressing HTTP communication as your main case, but you will also learn a lot of new tricks with Camel.

CHAPTER 2

Developing REST Integrations

In the last chapter, you were introduced to Apache Camel and Quarkus, you got started on the system integration discussion, and you learned a little bit about the evolution of the technologies approached by this book. This basic knowledge is extremely important to allow you to dive deeper into more specific conversations. Now, I'll discuss synchronous communication using REST.

Inter-process communication used to be a challenge for most developers. If we take the Java language as an example, during its development many mechanisms were created to allow different applications (different JVMs) to communicate between each other. We used to perform this communication using RMI (remote method invocation), straight up socket communication, or EJB remote invocation. Of course, during this evolution, we had implementations using HTTP. The JAX-RPC specification was a big step in standardizing HTTP-based communication using SOAP (Simple Object Access Protocol), an XML-based messaging protocol. JAX-RPC was eventually succeeded by the JAX-WS (Web Service) specification.

In the following years, SOAP was the primary choice when building web services. SOAP is an open-source, very descriptive, programming-language-agnostic protocol, making it a very good choice for web (HTTP) service implementations at the time. Even today you will find

G. Camposo, *Cloud Native Integration with Apache Camel*,
https://doi.org/10.1007/978-1-4842-7211-4_2

SOAP services deployed in traditional application services or sometimes microservices implementing SOAP to communicate with legacy systems.

A few years after SOAP was launched, Roy Fielding defined the REST (representational state transfer) architecture in his PhD dissertation. REST is not a messaging protocol, but a software architectural style that uses a subset of HTTP features. This means that we are not adding more complexity on the HTTP communication but defining a way of using HTTP for web service communication. This makes REST way lighter and simpler to implement than SOAP, besides being more applicable for a wider number of use cases, like web applications, mobile applications, and embedded systems.

We will discuss more about REST and HTTP in the upcoming chapters, but for now, let's start coding with Camel.

Camel DSLs

Camel is an extremely flexible framework. One example of its flexibility is the possibility to write Camel code in different ways that will suit different purposes. This is possible through Camel's different implementations of domain-specific languages (DSLs).

Camel implements the following types of DSL:

- Spring XML: An XML implementation based on Spring XML files

- Blueprint XML: An XML implementation based on OSGi Blueprint XML files

- Java DSL: The Java way to create routes. You used this approach in the first example.

- Rest DSL: A special way to define REST routes. It can be done with XML or Java.

- Annotation DSL: A way to interact with and create Camel objects using Java annotations.

I'm not covering all DSLs in this book. I will focus on the Java DSL and its complements, like the REST DSL for REST integrations.

Let's start by learning the REST DSL.

Examine the code in Listing 2-1, extracted from the second example, `camel-hello-world-restdsl`.

Listing 2-1. RestHelloWorldRoute.java File

```
package com.appress.integration;

import org.apache.camel.builder.RouteBuilder;

public class RestHelloWorldRoute extends RouteBuilder {
    @Override
    public void configure() throws Exception {

        rest("/helloWorld")
        .get()
            .route()
            .routeId("rest-hello-world")
            .setBody(constant("Hello World \n"))
            .log("Request responded with body: ${body}")
        .endRest();

    }
}
```

Before commenting on this code, let's test it. You can run this code using the following command:

```
camel-hello-world-restdsl $ mvn quarkus:dev
```

After this command, you should see Quarkus logs and have a log entry like this:

```
2021-04-21 12:58:33,758 INFO  [io.quarkus] (Quarkus Main
Thread) camel-rest-hello-world 1.0.0 on JVM (powered by
Quarkus 1.13.0.Final) started in 2.658s. Listening on: http://
localhost:8080
```

This means you have a web server running locally and listening on port 8080. You can test this app by running this command:

```
$ curl -w "\n" http://localhost:8080/helloWorld
```

The result should look like Figure 2-1.

```
~ $ curl -w "\n" http://localhost:8080/helloWorld
Hello World
```

Figure 2-1. *App response*

I'm using cURL, a tool normally found in Unix-like systems, as my command line HTTP client. You can use whatever tool you like to perform these tests. Just have cURL as a reference on which URL you should be pointing to and which arguments and parameters you should be setting.

Open this project in your favorite IDE. Examine it. You may notice some differences between the first example and this one. The first difference is that you have only one extension/dependency declared in your POM file, the camel-quarkus-rest. This happens because Camel extensions already declare the other extensions they depend on. For example, the camel-quarkus-core dependency is already declared by camel-quarkus-rest.

In this book's first example I wanted you to know that `camel-quarkus-core` is the base library for you to use Camel. From now on we don't need to explicitly declare it.

You can check what I said by running the command

`camel-hello-world-restdsl $ mvn dependency:tree`

The command above shows the project dependency tree. Besides the camel core dependency, I want you to pay attention to another dependency, `camel-quarkus-platform-http`. This dependency will allow you to use the web server implementation present in Quarkus. You may ask, which web server implementation, since we didn't declare anything. Well, if you look at the `quarkus-platform-http` dependencies, you see `quarkus-vertx-web`. This dependency is one of the web server implementations used by Quarkus. By declaring it this way, you inform Quarkus that you want to implement this specific web server module.

Another thing that is different from the first example is the way you are logging. You're not using `camel-quarkus-log` to provide a log endpoint. Instead, you're using the built-in fluent builder `log()`. Although `log()` is less flexible than using the log endpoint, it will serve just fine for your purpose of log messages per Exchanges. In the first example, I wanted you to know how the route structure works and I needed a simple endpoint to use in my `to()` invocation. That is why I chose the log endpoint. Behind the curtains, both implementations use the logging implementation from Quarkus, which in that case is `jboss-logging`.

In this example, I'm passing a string containing the message I want to display, but there is something that is dynamic in this string, the `${body}` marker. Do you remember when I talked about ELs? `${body}` is an example of an EL, in this case the Simple EL. So, depending on the body content, the message will change.

We will discuss logging and the Simple EL more in the future, but let's continue with the REST DSL explanation.

By analyzing the RestHelloWorldRoute class, the first thing you may notice is that there is no from() invocation. This happens because the REST DSL replaces the from() invocation by creating entries based on HTTP methods such as post(), put(), and delete(). You could even have multiple entries of the same method, if they had different paths.

You could also create REST services without using the REST DSL. Look at the code in the camel-hello-world-rest project. It does the exact same thing as hello-world-restdsl, but without the REST DSL. Let's analyze its RouteBuilder; see Listing 2-2.

Listing 2-2. RestHelloWorldRoute.java File

```java
package com.appress.integration;

import org.apache.camel.builder.RouteBuilder;

public class RestHelloWorldRoute extends RouteBuilder {
    @Override
    public void configure() throws Exception {
      from("platform-http:/helloWorld?httpMethodRestrict=GET")
        .routeId("rest-hello-world")
        .setBody(constant("Hello World"))
        .log("Request responded with body: ${body}");
    }
}
```

You can run and test this code the same way you did in the first example, and you will get the same result.

When you build REST services, normally you must create a resource that has different paths and works with different HTTP methods. Look at a more complex example in Listing 2-3.

Listing 2-3. TwoPathsRestRoute.java File

```java
public class TwoPathsRestRoute extends RouteBuilder {
    @Override
    public void configure() throws Exception {

        from("platform-http:/twoPaths/helloWorld?httpMethod
        Restrict=GET")
        .routeId("two-paths-hello")
        .setBody(constant("Hello World"))
        .log("Request responded with body: ${body}");

        from("platform-http:/twoPaths/sayHi?httpMethod
        Restrict=GET")
        .routeId("two-paths-hi")
        .setBody(constant("Hi"))
        .log("Request responded with body: ${body}");

    }
}
```

In order to expose two different paths, you had to create two different routes. This way you can define every aspect of each path independently. It is also the first time you are seeing a RouteBuilder producing more than one route. RouteBuilders can create multiple routes definitions. It is a matter of readability and semantics how many RouteBuilders you will have to create the routes you need.

This was a simple example to show you why you are going to use REST DSL and how to expose HTTP endpoints using Camel. REST DSL makes complex REST implementations easier and more readable. From now on you will use only REST DSL for REST resource declarations, and you are going to learn how to configure your interfaces properly.

REST and OpenAPI

When I started to talk about web services and I mentioned SOAP, one of the things I said that was interesting about the protocol was how descriptive it was. The specification allowed software and developers to understand how to make the web services calls, what data model was expected, how to handle authentication, and what would happen in error scenarios. These are things the HTTP protocol does not provide, so the community developed a way to make REST interfaces more descriptive and easier to interact with.

During the popularization of the REST architectural style, there were different attempts to create an interface description language to describe RESTful services (RESTful means that a service implements all the principals of the REST architectural style). It is safe to say that the most successful attempt was Swagger.

Created in 2011, Swagger is an open-source project that created a JSON/YAML representation for RESTful applications, taking many of the features built for the SOAP protocol. Besides the interface description language, Swagger also offered development tooling to facilitate API creation, testing, and visualization, from code generation based on documents to libraries to display web pages with Swagger documents based on the application code.

In 2016, the tooling and the specification were split, and the specification was renamed to OpenAPI.

OpenAPI, or OpenAPI Specification (OAS), is another open standard that you will adopt in this book. This facilitates how to work with many open source or proprietary software, because OpenAPI is a widely used standard and serves a common language.

Now that the introduction is done, you can start to develop some RESTful applications.

First Application: REST File Server

Enough with Hello World applications. It's time to see more complex applications that show more of Apache Camel's powers. There are some important Camel concepts that need to be discussed, but we will do so while analyzing a functional and testable code.

As a first application, I wanted something that would show much of the REST DSL configuration and requirements. Something that would go deeper in Camel's concepts but also something easy to understand and test. I came up with a solution that we used to do back in the days when we had to interact with applications that used the OS file system for inputting and outputting data.

Look at Figure 2-2.

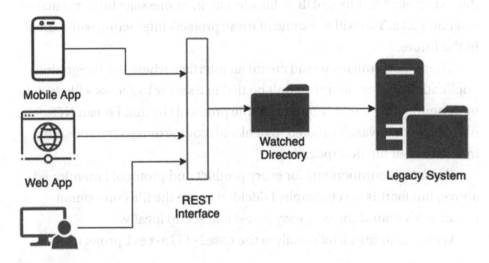

Figure 2-2. *REST File Server*

This integration abstracts the file system through a REST interface. This way other applications not hosted on the same server can send files to the legacy system using a more suitable communication protocol.

The integration exposes a REST interface to save files in the file system, so the legacy system can read them. It also allows the client to list which files are already saved in the server. We only care about the integration layer, more specifically the `camel-file-rest` project. So don't worry about running a legacy system on your machine.

When I said "back in the day" I meant that this situation is not very common nowadays. This is not because communication through files is something outdated, but we usually don't do it using simple OS file systems. However, I reckon that there are applications that still work this way.

A more cloud-native approach on file communication is to use more reliable and scalable mechanisms to send those files over. It could use object storage solutions such as AWS s3, document-orientated NoSQL databases such as MongoDB or Elasticsearch, or message brokers such as Apache Kafka. You will see some of these projects interacting with Camel in the future.

These mechanisms would create an interface where the integration application deployment wouldn't be tied to a server to access a file system or dependent on a non-atomic, reliable protocol (by that I mean NFS or FTP), or that wasn't tailored to deal with concurrency scenarios, file indexation, or file deduplication.

Camel has components for every product and protocol I mentioned above, but for this first example, I decided to use the file component because it's something very easy to test and set up locally.

With that in mind, let's analyze the `camel-file-rest` project.

REST Interfaces and OpenAPI

I discussed the importance of having a descriptive document for your interfaces. You are going to see how to generate OAS documents using Camel.

There are two ways to work with OpenAPI and Camel, much like when we used to work with SOAP web services. The first approach is top-down, where you first design your interface using the OpenAPI specification and then use it in your code to generate part of the implementation. You are not going to follow this approach here. My objective is to teach you how to solve integration problems and how to write Camel code. I want you to know that OpenAPI exists, that it is important, and how to use it with Camel. It is not my objective to dive deeper into the OpenAPI specification. Having said that, you'll go with the second approach, the bottom-up one where you use your code to generate your OpenAPI documentation.

First, let's start by analyzing the dependencies used in the camel-file-rest project. See Listing 2-4.

Listing 2-4. Camel-file-rest pom.xml Snippet

```
...
<dependencies>
    <dependency>
        <groupId>org.apache.camel.quarkus</groupId>
        <artifactId>camel-quarkus-rest</artifactId>
    </dependency>
    <dependency>
        <groupId>org.apache.camel.quarkus</groupId>
        <artifactId>camel-quarkus-file</artifactId>
    </dependency>
    <dependency>
        <groupId>org.apache.camel.quarkus</groupId>
        <artifactId>camel-quarkus-openapi-java</artifactId>
    </dependency>
    <dependency>
        <groupId>org.apache.camel.quarkus</groupId>
        <artifactId>camel-quarkus-direct</artifactId>
```

```
        </dependency>
        <dependency>
            <groupId>org.apache.camel.quarkus</groupId>
            <artifactId>camel-quarkus-bean</artifactId>
        </dependency>
        <dependency>
            <groupId>org.apache.camel.quarkus</groupId>
            <artifactId>camel-quarkus-jsonb</artifactId>
        </dependency>
    </dependencies>
...
```

The camel-quarkus-rest dependency is not new. You used it in the
Hello World REST example. You are using it to provide the REST DSL
capabilities to your routes. You are going to use camel-quarkus-file to
use the file: endpoint. It will allow you to save files with minimal effort.
The camel-quarkus-openapi-java will generate the OpenAPI document
for you. There are three other dependencies to comment about, but I will
do that later, when we talk about how they affect the code. First, let's focus
on the interface declaration.

Look at the FileServerRoute class and its configure() method,
shown in Listing 2-5.

Listing 2-5. FileServerRoute.class Configure Method

```
@Override
public void configure() throws Exception {
    createFileServerApiDefinition();
    createFileServerRoutes();
}
```

Here I separated the code that defines the interface of your REST
application from the code that implements the integration with the file system.

This way you can focus on parts of the code and discuss its content separately. Look at createFileServerApiDefinition() in Listing 2-6.

Listing 2-6. createFileServerApiDefinition Method

```
private void createFileServerApiDefinition(){
  restConfiguration()
    .apiContextPath("/fileServer/doc")
    .apiProperty("api.title", "File Server API")
    .apiProperty("api.version","1.0.0")
    .apiProperty("api.description", "REST API to save files");

  rest("/fileServer")
   .get("/file")
     .id("get-files")
     .description("Generates a list of saved files")
     .produces(MEDIA_TYPE_APP_JSON)
     .responseMessage().code(200).endResponseMessage()
     .responseMessage().code(204)
       .message(CODE_204_MESSAGE).endResponseMessage()
     .responseMessage().code(500)
     .message(CODE_500_MESSAGE).endResponseMessage()
     .to(DIRECT_GET_FILES)

   .post("/file")
     .id("save-file")
     .description("Saves the HTTP Request body into a File,
     using the fileName header to set the file name. ")
     .consumes(MEDIA_TYPE_TEXT_PLAIN)
     .produces(MEDIA_TYPE_TEXT_PLAIN)
     .responseMessage().code(201)
       .message(CODE_201_MESSAGE).endResponseMessage()
     .responseMessage().code(500)
```

51

```
        .message(CODE_500_MESSAGE).endResponseMessage()
    .to(DIRECT_SAVE_FILE);
}
```

The restConfiguration() method is responsible for configurations related to how Camel connects with the underlying web server (Quarkus Web Server). You are not doing much since you are relying on the default configuration, but you are setting the path where you want the OAS document to be displayed by calling apiContextPath() and adding information for the generated document by calling apiProperty().

From the rest() calling onwards you are describing your resource methods and paths, declaring what kind of data is expected, what kind of response will be given, and how this interface is supposed to work.

Before diving into the implementation, let's see what this first part of the code does. Run the application as follows:

```
camel-file-rest $ mvn quarkus:dev
```

To retrieve the generated document, you could use the following command:

```
$ curl http://localhost:8080/fileServer/doc
```

You could also use your favorite web browser, accessing the same URL. Either way, you should receive the JSON document shown in Listing 2-7.

Listing 2-7. OAS-Generated Document

```
{
  "openapi" : "3.0.2",
  "info" : {
    "title" : "File Server API",
    "version" : "1.0.0",
    "description" : "REST API to save files"
  },
```

```
"servers" : [ {
  "url" : ""
} ],
"paths" : {
  "/fileServer/file" : {
    "get" : {
      "tags" : [ "fileServer" ],
      "responses" : {
        "200" : {
          "description" : "success"
        },
        "204" : {
          "description" : "No files found on the server."
        },
        "500" : {
          "description" : "Something went wrong on the server side."
        }
      },
      "operationId" : "get-files",
      "summary" : "Generates a list of files present in
      the server"
    },
    "post" : {
      "tags" : [ "fileServer" ],
      "responses" : {
        "201" : {
          "description" : "File created on the server."
        },
        "500" : {
          "description" : "Something went wrong on the server
          side."
        }
```

```
      },
      "operationId" : "save-file",
      "summary" : "Saves the HTTP Request body into a File,
      using the fileName header to set the file name. "
    }
  }
},
"tags" : [ {
  "name" : "fileServer"
} ]
}
```

Notice the "openapi" attribute. Its value is "3.0.2". This means you are using OpenAPI specification version 3, which was released in 2017. Since this is a fairly new version, you may still find documents in version 2. By the way, this is the first version where the specification changed its name from Swagger Specification to Open API Specification (OAS).

My intention with this section was to introduce you to OAS and teach you how to write Camel RESTful integrations, but if you are looking for more information on OAS, visit the OpenAPI Initiative website at www.openapis.org/.

Readability and Logic Reuse

At this point, you are not dealing with the complexity of adapting the communication between two different endpoints. You are focusing on learning Camel's principles and how to write integration routes. Now you'll start to add more complexity as the examples start to have more endpoints and you'll add more logic for its integration. To deal with this complexity, there are some techniques you can use to keep your routes easy to read and maintain.

You started this book by using two very simple endpoints: the timer and the log components. There were little configuration options related to these components, but they were used to illustrate how Camel works in a simplified way. Now you have a more complex situation on your hands. You need to transform an HTTP request into a file and give back an HTTP response.

Let's check how this is done by looking at how you list the files. See Listing 2-8.

Listing 2-8. createFileServerApiDefinition Method Snippet

```
...
  .post("/file")
    .id("save-file")
    .description("Saves the HTTP Request body into a File,
    using the fileName header to set the file name. ")
    .consumes(MEDIA_TYPE_TEXT_PLAIN)
    .produces(MEDIA_TYPE_TEXT_PLAIN)
    .responseMessage().code(201)
.message(CODE_201_MESSAGE).endResponseMessage()
    .responseMessage().code(500).message(CODE_500_MESSAGE)
.endResponseMessage()
    .to(DIRECT_SAVE_FILE);
...
```

Focusing in the POST method declaration above, you can see that there is no complete route definition here, but you do have a to() call using a static variable. Let's look the variable declaration:

```
public static final String DIRECT_SAVE_FILE = "direct:save-file";
```

Although each HTTP method declaration, with your respective path, will always generate a route, you're not declaring the whole route in this single fluent builder structure. To facilitate the code readability and help with my mission, which is to explain things in small pieces, I decided to use the direct component.

The direct component allows you to link, synchronously, different routes in the same Camel context. The Camel context is a new concept in the Camel architecture that you are going to explore right now.

Run the application again. Look for a log entry like this:

```
(Quarkus Main Thread) Apache Camel 3.9.0 (camel-1) started in
128ms (build:0ms init:86ms start:42ms)
```

You may wonder what camel-1 means. Well, that is your Camel context. During the application runtime startup process, Camel will create a structure of objects so the integrations may run. During this process, Java beans are created, your routes and configuration are loaded, and everything is associated to a specific context, so those objects can share data between each other and inherit the same configurations.

For now, you are not going to do any specific configuration with the Camel context. I just want you to know that this concept exists, and you need your routes in the same context to use the direct component. In the way you are working every route will be created in the same context.

Going back to the direct component analysis, you saw how it looks from the producer perspective (the to() call). Let's see how it goes on the consumer side (from()). Look at the createSaveFileRoute() method in Listing 2-9.

Listing 2-9. createSaveFileRoute Method

```
private void createSaveFileRoute() throws URISyntaxException{
  from(DIRECT_SAVE_FILE)
    .routeId("save-file")
    .setHeader(Exchange.FILE_NAME,simple("${header.fileName}"))
    .to("file:"+ FileReaderBean.getServerDirURI())
    .setHeader(Exchange.HTTP_RESPONSE_CODE, constant(201))
    .setHeader(Exchange.CONTENT_TYPE,
                          constant(MEDIA_TYPE_TEXT_PLAIN))
    .setBody(constant(CODE_201_MESSAGE)) ;
}
```

The same static variable defines the producer and the consumer just to facilitate this explanation. Keep in mind that there are different options for producers and consumers, but you're not using them right now. Besides the direct, you're using the Simple EL to dynamically retrieve the file name from the POST request header and using a static method to retrieve the directory name to where you are going to save the files. Look at the FileReaderBean class, getServerDirURI() method in Listing 2-10.

Listing 2-10. getServerDirURI Method

```
public static String getServerDirURI() throws
URISyntaxException{
    return Paths.get(FileReaderBean.class.getResource("/")
            .toURI()).getParent()+ "/camel-file-rest-dir";
}
```

You're using the project Maven's generated target folder to save the files. This way you don't need to configure anything in your system, and you can also clean your test by simply running "mvn clean".

It is important to notice that I'm using a very "optimistic" development approach here. I'm not treating any possible exception. At this point, the idea is to keep things as simple as possible. This way we can focus on a particular subject of study. You will learn how to handle exceptions with Camel and other patterns for alternative execution flows in future chapters.

To go further in the direct component explanation, let's analyze a different code that uses direct for code reuse. Open the camel-direct-log project in your IDE. Look at the DirectTestRoute class configure() method, shown in Listing 2-11.

Listing 2-11. DirectTest Route Configure Method

```
public void configure() throws Exception {
    rest("/directTest")
        .post("/path1")
            .id("path1")
            .route()
                .to("log:path1-logger")
                .to("direct:logger")
                .setBody(constant("path1"))
            .endRest()
        .post("/path2")
            .id("path2")
            .route()
                .to("log:path2-logger")
                .to("direct:logger")
                .setBody(constant("path2"))
            .endRest();

    from("direct:logger")
        .routeId("logger-route")
        .to("log:logger-route?showAll=true");
}
```

The code above doesn't do much. It's a REST interface that logs the incoming data and returns a constant response. The focal point here is how two different routes can link to a third route to reuse its logic.

Run the code like this:

```
camel-direct-log $ mvn quarkus:dev
```

You can test the application by running

```
$ curl http://localhost:8080/directTest/path1 -X POST -H
'Content-Type: text/plain' --data-raw 'Test!'
```

Look at the application logs. For each Exchange you will find two log entries like Listing 2-12.

Listing 2-12. camel-direct-log Logs

```
2021-05-01 17:03:36,858 INFO [path1-logger] (vert.x-worker-
thread-2) Exchange[ExchangePattern: InOut, BodyType: io.vertx.
core.buffer.impl.BufferImpl, Body: Test!]
2021-05-01 17:03:36,859 INFO [logger-route] (vert.x-worker-
thread-2) Exchange[Id: B23C7938FE44124-0000000000000005,
ExchangePattern: InOut, Properties: {}, Headers: {Accept=*/*,
CamelHttpMethod=POST, CamelHttpPath=/directTest/path1,
CamelHttpQuery=null, CamelHttpRawQuery=null, CamelHttpUri=/
directTest/path1, CamelHttpUrl=http://localhost:8080/
directTest/path1, Content-Length=5, Content-Type=text/plain,
Host=localhost:8080, User-Agent=curl/7.54.0}, BodyType:
io.vertx.core.buffer.impl.BufferImpl, Body: Test!]
```

Every time a request is done for the `path1`, two log entries will be created, one for the `path1-route` route and another one for the `logger-route`. The default log formatter used in the examples uses the following format:

```
${date-time} ${log level} ${logger name} ${thread name} ${log content}
```

The logs are different because the `logger-route` route is setting the `showAll` parameter to true, which means that the whole exchange object

will be printed. You could test the path2 too and you would get
similar results.

```
$ curl http://localhost:8080/directTest/path2 -X POST \
-H 'Content-Type: text/plain' --data-raw 'Test!'
```

The path1-route and path2-route implement the same logic, and
both use the logger-route, but what I want you to see is that even though
each exchange produces logs in different routes, the path-router and
the logger- router, they are executed in the same thread because of
the direct component. Look at the log entries; both are printing (vert.x-
worker-thread-2) as the thread name because they were executed in the
same thread.

Consumers normally have a thread pool in order to process multiple
exchanges at once. In this case, you are using the Vertx web library to
implement an HTTP web server. Vertx uses a reactive approach in order
to make better use of computing resources, by following an asynchronous
non-blocking IO execution model, even though it allocates multiple
threads for event looping and worker threads.

Direct allows you to aggregate a routing logic to another route. This
way you can reuse a routing logic in more than one route. This was a very
simplistic example of how to use direct to reuse logic or improve code
readability, but it served the purpose of explaining how it works and
expanding on other Camel concepts.

Let's get back to the camel-file-rest project.

Beans and Processors

Components are a huge tool to abstract implementations complexities,
but there are situations where they might not be enough. You may not
find the right component for your necessity, you may want to do a simple
processing, or maybe you want to do a really complex processing and

doing it in the route is just not possible. Camel offers different ways to deal with these cases. Let's see some of the possibilities.

Look back at the `FileServerRoute` class in the `camel-file-rest` project, more precisely, in the `createGetFilesRoute()` method, shown in Listing 2-13.

Listing 2-13. createGetFilesRoute Method

```
private void createGetFilesRoute(){
  from(DIRECT_GET_FILES)
  .routeId("get-files")
  .log("getting files list")
  .bean(FileReaderBean.class, "listFile")
  .choice()
  .when(simple("${body} != null"))
      .marshal().json(JsonLibrary.Jsonb);
}
```

There are some new concepts to explore in this route, but first let's analyze why you need the `FileReaderBean` class.

You might remember this class from your other route, where you used its static method `getServerDirURI()` to retrieve the server directory URI and set its value in the file component configuration. You are also using this class to list the files present in the server. You need to do this because the file component works in a specific way that will not fit for this case.

Components might act as consumers or producers, and in some cases, as both. To be clear, a consumer in the Camel universe means you are connected to a resource, such as a database, a file system, a message broker, and others. It could also mean that you are exposing a service and consuming the incoming data, as you do with the `camel-quarkus-platform-http` component in the REST integration. It allows you to expose a REST service and receive requests.

A producer, on the other hand, is a component that sends or persists data to another endpoint. A producer can also send data to a database, a file system, a message broker, and more. It really depends on how the component works. In your case, the file component does work as a consumer and a producer, but not exactly how you need.

Your route starts with a REST interface (consumer) and it calls another route through the direct component. From there you need to find a way to list the server directory, but the file component, as a producer (to()), does not provide a way to query a directory. It only persists files. You solve this problem by implementing the logic in a Java bean class called FileReaderBean and you call it using the fluent builder bean(), passing the class you want to use and the method you need.

Look at the FileReaderBean implementation of the listFile() method in Listing 2-14.

Listing 2-14. FileReader Bean listFile Method

```
public void listFile(Exchange exchange) throws URISyntaxException {

  File serverDir = new File(getServerDirURI());
    if (serverDir.exists()){

        List<String> fileList = new ArrayList<>();

        for (File file : serverDir.listFiles()){
          fileList.add(file.getName());
        }

        if(!fileList.isEmpty()){
           LOG.info("setting list of files");
           exchange.getMessage().setBody(fileList);
        }else{
           LOG.info("no files found");
        }
```

```
    }else{
        LOG.info("no files created yet");
    }
}
```

This method uses the Java IO library to interact with the file system and list the files of a given directory. This is nothing new for a Java developer. What is new is how this logic interacts with the Camel route.

The main thing to notice is that this method receives a Camel exchange object as an argument. If you look at the route, you are not setting arguments for the bean invocation, and you don't need to. Camel's binding process can determine which method to invoke based on how the methods are declared or how you set the bean invocation. You could, for example, remove the parameter `"listFiles"` from the `bean(FileReaderBean.class, "listFile")` invocation and it would still work because of the way the `FileReaderBean` is implemented, where only the `listFile()` method would be a fit for this invocation.

The Exchange object is not the only object automatically bind in a bean invocation. You could also use

- `org.apache.camel.Message`

- `org.apache.camel.CamelContext`

- `org.apache.camel.TypeConverter`

- `org.apache.camel.spi.Registry`

- `java.lang.Exception`

I went for the Exchange plus "void return" pattern because my intention was to change the Exchange's message object and affect the route response. For this particular case, I could also use the Message object binding, because I'm not accessing any other Exchange's properties, but I just want to give you a broader example for your future reference.

Another thing worth mentioning is how we are accessing the bean object. Beans can be invoked by their names, as they are registered in the bean registry. I could have passed a string with the bean's name and Camel would have found the right object, if I had registered it using the CDI specification. I also could have passed one object instance to be used by the route. Since my code is pretty simple, I chose to simplify my approach and pass the class that I needed and let Camel instantiate and handle the object for me.

Beans can be accessed using the beans() fluent builder or using the bean component, in that case making reference to bean: endpoint. As you can see, there are many ways to reuse and encapsulate your code logic within Camel, but there are also ways to insert more localized processing logic. One way of doing it is by using Processors.

Listing 2-15 shows how the get-files route would be if you used a Processor instead.

Listing 2-15. createGetFilesRoute Method with Processor

```
private void createGetFilesRoute(){
from(DIRECT_GET_FILES)
.routeId("get-files")
.log("getting files list")
.process(new Processor() {
@Override
public void process(Exchange exchange) throws Exception {
  File serverDir = new File(FileReaderBean.getServerDirURI());
        if (serverDir.exists()){
            List<String> fileList = new ArrayList<>();
            for (File file : serverDir.listFiles()){
                fileList.add(file.getName());
            }
            if(!fileList.isEmpty()){
```

```
            exchange.getMessage().setBody(fileList);
        }
    }
}
})
.choice()
.when(simple("${body} != null"))
    .marshal().json(JsonLibrary.Jsonb);
}
```

`Processor` is an interface that declares a single method, `process(Exchange exchange)`. In this example, you're implementing it using an anonymous inner class. This is the easiest way to input some processing logic in your route, but it is not reusable. If you want to reuse this code, you could also implement the interface in a separate class and pass an instance to the route `process()` call.

I usually use beans to do processing. Beans do not require a specific interface and are a broader concept in the Java language. This way I can keep my code more portable and readable for other Java developers who are not that familiar with Camel.

I wanted you to know the two approaches, `Processors` and beans, as you may find both in your future adventures with Camel. Let's continue with the code deconstruction.

Predicates

When thinking about a routing logic, there are situations that may have conditional steps. Due to the incoming data, you may need to choose a specific route. You can incorporate conditional steps in your routing logic using predicates.

Going back to the `get-files` route, you have a step that will only be executed if a specific condition is met. You start the construction by calling the choice() method, which can specify many different options using the when() method and even set an option that is only met when every other option fail, using otherwise(). Every option is analyzed by running an expression language predicate that must return a Boolean result.

In the example presented in the get-files route, the last line of code will only be executed if the body of the message is not null. If you remember the listFile() method in the FileReaderBean class, a body will only be set if there is a file in the directory. For your REST component, a response with a null body and no exceptions means that the request was successful, but no content was found, therefore the HTTP status code should be 204.

Let's try this scenario. Run the following command to clean the directory and start the application:

```
camel-file-rest $ mvn clean quarkus:dev
```

To test the get-files route, you can run the following command:

```
$ curl -v http://localhost:8080/fileServer/file
```

Use -v to get a verbose response with cURL. This way you can see clearly what the HTTP status code in the response is, as you can see in Figure 2-3.

```
~ $ curl -v http://localhost:8080/fileServer/file
*    Trying ::1...
* TCP_NODELAY set
* Connection failed
* connect to ::1 port 8080 failed: Connection refused
*    Trying 127.0.0.1...
* TCP_NODELAY set
* Connected to localhost (127.0.0.1) port 8080 (#0)
> GET /fileServer/file HTTP/1.1
> Host: localhost:8080
> User-Agent: curl/7.54.0
> Accept: */*
>
< HTTP/1.1 204 No Content
< Accept: */*
< User-Agent: curl/7.54.0
< Content-Type: application/json
<
* Connection #0 to host localhost left intact
```

Figure 2-3. *No content response*

Before you analyze the last line of code in the get-file route, let's see
another example of how to use predicates. Open the camel-rest-choice
project in your favorite IDE. This project creates a single REST route that
returns a salute based on the HTTP request parameters. Look at the route
created in the RestChoiceRoute class in Listing 2-16.

Listing 2-16. RestChoiceRoute Configure Method

```
public void configure() throws Exception {

rest("/RestChoice")
.get()
.id("rest-choice")
.produces("text/plain")
.route()
.choice()
```

67

```
.when(header("preferred_title").isEqualToIgnoreCase("mrs"))
   .setBody(simple("Hi Mrs. ${header.name}"))
.when(header("preferred_title").isEqualToIgnoreCase("mr"))
   .setBody(simple("Hi Mr. ${header.name}"))
.when(header("preferred_title").isEqualToIgnoreCase("ms"))
   .setBody(simple("Hi Ms. ${header.name}"))
.otherwise()
   .setBody(simple("Hey ${header.name}"));
}
```

Here is an example of how to use the choice structure to create a multiple option scenario. You are also using otherwise(), which allows you to set a default option in case any of the previous options are not met. You are using the Header EL to evaluate the decisions based on the header content in the HTTP request.

Let's test this code. Run the application with the following command:

```
camel-rest-choice $ mvn quarkus:dev
```

In another terminal, you may test the application with the following command:

```
$ curl -w "\n" http://localhost:8080/RestChoice?name=John \
-H "preferred_title: mr"
```

The response for this call will be "Hi Mr. John" because you are using "mr" as the preferred title. If you didn't send the "preferred_title" header or you set it using an unexpected value, the response would be "Hey John", because the otherwise() option would be met.

As you can see, you can use EL predicates to evaluate conditions in your choice structure. Although the expression languages are very flexible, there are situations where you may have more complex variables to evaluate. In those cases, you may implement an interface to create a customizable predicate.

Data Formats

For this particular REST interface, you are working with two different media types: text/plain and application/json. The use of text/plain is convenient because when you translate this into the Java language, you will be dealing with Strings, which is a simple-to-use and very complete data structure, but normally you need to deal with more high-level objects that represent your data structure.

Go back to the `get-files` route in the `camel-file-rest` project. The following line of code was left to explain:

```
marshal().json(JsonLibrary.Jsonb);
```

If you remember, your REST interface should return a JSON object as a response for the `get-files` method, but the `FileReaderBean` method, `listFile()`, only returns a list of names in a Java format. That's why you need to convert the message body to a JSON format.

Usually when you need to work with data structures in Java, you tend to represent those structures with POJO (plain old Java object) classes, simplifying binary data into String or byte arrays and transforming this data into something easy to refer to when programming. When you think about JSON or XML and you want to manipulate its content, it is a common approach to parse its content to a POJO. Using libraries as JAXB or JSON-B you can transform Java objects into XML/JSON or transform the Java object into an XML/JSON document.

XML and JSON are not the only data formats that are commonly used. Camel offers a great deal of formats to work with, including

- YAML

- CSV

- Avro

- Zip file

- Base64

- and others

In this example, you are marshalling the data, which means transforming a Java object structure into a binary or textual format. You could also do the opposite and unmarshall() a binary or textual format into a Java object.

To deal with the JSON data format, which will be heavily used in your REST integrations, you will use JSON-B as your parser, as it is the standard implementation for the MicroProfile specification.

You will see data formats in different contexts in future chapters. For now, let's look to a more low-level type of data conversion.

Type Converters

The example application receives a HTTP request and persists it into a file in the server file system. You only wrote a few lines of code where you describe the type of interface you want to use and point it to where you want to save the files. There is a lot happening between these steps, and that is the beauty of Camel: you can do a lot with a few lines of code. I want you to understand what happens behind the scenes, so you can make the right choice when building your routes.

Let's look back at the part of the code that saves the file in the file system. See Listing 2-17.

Listing 2-17. createSaveFileRoute Method

```
private void createSaveFileRoute() throws URISyntaxException{
  from(DIRECT_SAVE_FILE)
  .routeId("save-file")
  .setHeader(Exchange.FILE_NAME, simple("${header.fileName}"))
  .to("file:"+ FileReaderBean.getServerDirURI())
```

```
.setHeader(Exchange.HTTP_RESPONSE_CODE, constant(201))
.setHeader(Exchange.CONTENT_TYPE,
  constant(MEDIA_TYPE_TEXT_PLAIN))
.setBody(constant(CODE_201_MESSAGE)) ;
}
```

The only thing needed to save the request as a file is to extract the file name from a header parameter. Let's run the application and save a file. First start the application:

camel-file-rest $ mvn clean quarkus:dev

You can create a file like this:

```
$ curl -X POST http://localhost:8080/fileServer/file -H
'fileName: test.txt' -H 'Content-Type: text/plain' --data-raw
'this is my file content'
```

You may want to check if the file is there. You can look at the project's target folder (camel-file-rest/target/camel-file-rest-dir) or just run the list file call:

```
$ curl http://localhost:8080/fileServer/file
```

Data conversion or transformation is something that happens all the time in Camel routes. This usually happens because each component or endpoint work with a specific type of data.

Take the camel-rest-file application as an example. The incoming data is treated by a Java web server as a stream of bytes sequentially sent over the network. To abstract this process, Java utilizes libraries to perform the IO operations, and specifically talking about reading data, it usually uses the InputStream class to read data in the file system or data coming through the network. The same thing happens when you send data or write it to the file system. Java also has a representation for writing streams of bytes, the OutputStream.

There are other objects used in Java to represent, let's say, more low-level data structures. Camel acknowledges those objects or primitives and handles their manipulation through a structure called a **type converter**. Here is a list of the types handled by default in Camel:

- File

- String

- byte[] and Bytebuffer

- InputStream and OutputStream

- Reader and Writer

- Document and Source

Beside the types already present, you can also implement your own converters, using the TypeConverters interface. Let's analyze how a converter implementation works. Open the camel-type-converter project. Look at the TypeConverterTimerRoute class and see the created route. See Listing 2-18.

Listing 2-18. TypeConverterTimerRoute Configure Method

```
public void configure() throws Exception {

from("timer:type-converter-timer?period=2000")
.routeId("type-converter-route")
.process(new Processor() {
    @Override
    public void process(Exchange exchange) throws Exception {
        MyObject object = new MyObject();
        object.setValue(UUID.randomUUID().toString());
        exchange.getMessage().setBody(object);
    }
})
```

```
.convertBodyTo(AnotherObject.class)
.log("${body}");

}
```

This is a very simple route, just to show how conversion works. For this example, there are two POJO classes, MyObject and AnotherObject, which have a single attribute called value. The main difference between the two classes is that AnotherObject implements the toString() method to make the resulting string show the object attribute values. The most significant part of the route is when you explicitly ask for a conversion calling convertBodyTo() and pass, as an argument, the class you want the object to be converted to, AnotherObject.class. As you can see, there is no explicit declaration in the route on how this conversion must be done, but it is something discovered at runtime.

Look at the MyObjectConverter class in Listing 2-19.

Listing 2-19. MyObjectConverter.java File

```
@Singleton
@Unremovable
public class MyObjectConverter implements TypeConverters {

@Converter
public static AnotherObject toAnotherObject(MyObject object){

        AnotherObject anotherObject = new AnotherObject();
        anotherObject.setValue(object.getValue());

        return anotherObject;
    }
}
```

MyObjectConverter is a bean because it is annotated with @Singleton, which means that a single instance of this object will be created and

maintained by the bean registry. This class also implements the
TypeConverters interface, which does not have any method declaration
but serves to make this object discoverable. This class has a single static
method annotated as @Converter, with a specific return class and a
specific object as a parameter, which makes this method adequate to be
discovered in a conversion process.

You may also have noticed the @Unremovable annotation. This is not
directly connected with the Camel implementation, but it is related to
how code is prepared by the Quarkus plugin when compiling. Do you
remember that Quarkus anticipates a few runtime processes? One
of them is to validate how CDI is used by the code. Since there is no
explicit reference of any class injecting this bean, Quarkus removes
this class from the loading process. To avoid this behavior, one
possible solution is to annotate the class with @Unremovable. You
may try to remove this annotation and see what happens when trying
to execute the application. Sometimes causing errors can be a great
way to learn.

As other object structures, converters are also maintained under the
Camel context, more specifically, in the Type Converter Registry. As the
bean instance is created by the framework, Camel can discover it because
of the interface use and add it to the Type Converter Registry. So, when
body conversion is needed, Camel can check the registry for the converter
that is a right fit.

To test this application, just run the following command:

```
camel-type-converter $ mvn quarkus:dev
```

At this point you should start seeing log entries like Listing 2-20.

Listing 2-20. camel-type-converter Logs

```
2021-05-10 08:53:04,915 INFO  [type-converter-route]
(Camel (camel-1) thread #0 - timer://type-converter-timer)
AnotherObject{value='2090187e-0df7-4126-b610-fa7f92790cde'}
2021-05-10 08:53:06,900 INFO  [type-converter-route]
(Camel (camel-1) thread #0 - timer://type-converter-timer)
AnotherObject{value='deab51df-75b1-4437-a605-bda2f7f21708'}
```

Since you are setting MyObject with random UUIDs, every log entry will vary, but this way it is clear that you are in fact calling the toString() method of the AnotherObject class.

Summary

This chapter introduced how to expose REST web services with Camel, but it also went deeper into Camel concepts.

You learned about the following:

- The different ways to write Camel routes

- Web services evolution through the years

- What REST is about

- A new open standard with OpenAPI

- How to improve code readability and reuse code

- How to include programming logic in your routes

- How Camel deals with different data structures and formats

Now you have a better overall understanding of how Camel works. You saw a lot of code but now you are ready to look at more complex code examples, especially dealing with more than one application at once.

In the next chapter, you will explore application communication with REST and Web Service security.

CHAPTER 3

Securing Web Services with Keycloak

We have been talking about web services, how the approaches evolved, and how to write web services, but there is a very important topic when we are talking about exposing services on the Internet that I didn't mention: security.

Of course, security is one topic in the web services theme, but it is also a theme on its own. I will talk about some overall security concepts, but have in mind that this chapter's objective is not to broadly explain security, but to teach you how to deal with some commonly found security needs or protocols when you are writing integrations using Apache Camel.

When we talk about security on the Web, we are talking about how to make access to web services or web applications secure. There are different things that we have to take into consideration to have the security aspect of our application covered. First, we need to secure the communication channel. When we are talking about a partner or consumer in our own organization, we may create VPNs (virtual private networks) that will mask our data and our IP routing. This mechanism is very secure and optimal for scenarios where we know exactly who is accessing our application, but is not applicable for services that target

G. Camposo, *Cloud Native Integration with Apache Camel*,
https://doi.org/10.1007/978-1-4842-7211-4_3

an open audience on the Internet. For the second scenario, we usually rely on TLS to encrypt our HTTP connection to secure the data being transferred through the Internet. HTTPS (the combination of TLS + HTTP) protects us from man-in-the-middle attacks, where a hacker could be eavesdropping on the connection to steal data or tamper with the data in order to attack the server or the client.

There are other possible attacks such as injections, cross-site scripting, directory traversal, DDoS, and so on. It is extremely important to protect your services from the listed attacks. Most of them won't be handled by your service but by specialized software that intermediate the connection between your client and your service, like a web application firewall (WAF).

In this chapter, you will explore access control, which also is a fundamental aspect of service security. You will see how to expose REST APIs and protect them using well-established open standard authentication and authorization protocols and also how to consume APIs using the same protocols.

Access Control

One commonly found necessity in web services is to have service responses based on who is asking for the data. This may mean that this data is private and should be only accessed by its owner and because of that the service must be able to identify who is making the request and check if that entity should be entitled to access the requested data. There are other scenarios where we might have data that is for public consumption or that is relevant or owned by a group, but either way, in order to provide these functionalities we need tooling to allow us to perform access control.

Think about the majority of applications or systems that you have to interact with in your life. I wouldn't be surprised that your user experience started by entering a username and a password on a login screen. Having a username and password or a key and secret pair is the most common way to authenticate a user or a system. To be clear on the concept, authentication means "to identify if the provided user and his credentials (in this case the password) are valid for that particular system."

Being identified is normally one step explored by access control. Most systems or applications have exclusive content based on user attributes, groups they might belong to, or roles applied to them. Once the user tries to access specific content, the access control has to check if the user is authorized to access that content. In that sense, authorization means "the act of verifying if a given entity has the permission to access data or to perform an action in the system."

As you can see, *authentication* and *authorization* are two different concepts that are intrinsically interconnected. They form the basis of how we build access control to our applications. There are different ways to authenticate a user and different ways to deal with authorization. Let's discuss some protocols.

OAuth 2.0

What if we could have an open industry-standard protocol to describe how our authorization flows should work? This is the case with OAuth 2.0. Let's see what this protocol is about.

We are more connected than ever, and all this connectivity depends on web applications and web services. When I say web applications I mean applications developed for use in web browsers. Web services are the non-visual, non-browser-oriented APIs that feed other web services, mobile applications, desktop applications, and so on. To access all those services and applications, we depend on the authentication and authorization of users. If we go back a few years in time, we would have the following scenario for a given web application:

> *Once the user logged into the application, a session would be created for him to maintain his information on the server side and also to keep track of the data he was generating while utilizing the system. If somehow the user unintentionally dropped the browser and lost the local reference for that session, he would have to reenter his username and password to get back into the application. The server side could try to retrieve the session information or create a new one and eventually drop the "orphan" one from memory.*

There are few applications designed like this nowadays because this approach has a lot of problems. The main one is how poorly it scales. To maintain in-memory session information on the server side is extremely taxing on server resources when we think about having millions of users accessing our application. Of course, there is still the necessity of having some in-memory information about connections or the overall server side status, but the strategy now is to try to share this load as much as possible with the client side. Web applications now rely heavily on cookies to store and persist users' session states on the client side and the use of REST APIs, which are stateless services by nature. It's natural that our access control mechanism would evolve to also fit better in this scenario.

At this point, we need to break apart the notion of *identity and authentication* from the notion of *authorization and access granting*. You will understand why in a moment.

OAuth is an open standard protocol designed to specify how access granting flow (authorization) should happen. Its development started in 2006 in a joint effort of Twitter and Gnolia, which was implementing OpenID authentication for its websites at that moment.

OpenID is also an open standard but it is focused on authentication. It intends to solve a common problem in today's world: having to handle many users and passwords for different systems. People are consuming many different services on the Internet. From video streaming platforms to social media, we are connected to many different websites and each of them has its identity database where we need to create our user. Life could be way simpler if we could have our identity information in a separate system and use it to authenticate in different systems. That is what OpenID is about. It's a single point for authentication that can be used for various systems.

I said that we need to separate the authentication and authorization concepts because in our case they are handled by different protocol specifications. OpenID is responsible for the authentication and OAuth for authorization. For now, let's focus on OAuth and authorization.

In order to understand how OAuth helps with access granting, you need to understand OAuth's flows, but before that you need to understand the roles defined by the specification. Look at Figure 3-1.

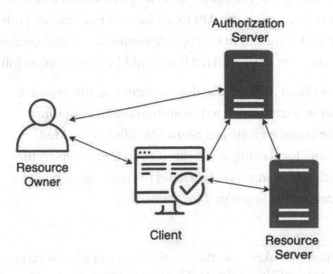

Figure 3-1. *OAuth role interaction*

OAuth is something very present in our relationship with services on the Internet. Take social login, where you can log on to a given website using your user account from social media such as Facebook, GitHub, Google, and so on. They all use OAuth as the protocol. Take this example to understand the roles:

You just found a very interesting website that allows you to edit photos in your Facebook photo albums. It requires you to log in using your Facebook account, so you have to give permission to the website to access some of your Facebook data. Once the permissions are given, you will be able to edit your photos and save them in your Facebook photo album.

In this case, you are the **resource owner** because you own the data (photos, profile information, and so on). The website you are accessing is the client that redirects you to Facebook for authentication and authorization. Once you are logged in on Facebook and have the right set of permissions, the client will access your data on your behalf. Facebook is the authorization server and the resource server. It is an authorization server because it is responsible for identifying you and issuing a signed token that contains enough information to identify you and the permissions for the client to act on your behalf. It is also a resource server because it provides the API to access and manipulate your photo album and check if the client is properly authorized based on the token information they are passing. This flow could be described as follows[1]:

1. The client initiates the flow by directing the resource owner's user-agent to the authorization endpoint. The client includes its client identifier, requested scope, local state, and a redirection URI to which the authorization server will send the user-agent back once access is granted (or denied).

---

[1] This description was taken from the OAuth 2.0 specification at `https://datatracker.ietf.org/doc/html/rfc6749#section-4.1`

2.   The authorization server authenticates the resource owner (via the user-agent) and establishes whether the resource owner grants or denies the client's access request.

3.   Assuming the resource owner grants access, the authorization server redirects the user-agent back to the client using the redirection URI provided earlier (in the request or during client registration). The redirection URI includes an authorization code and any local state provided by the client earlier.

4.   The client requests an access token from the authorization server's token endpoint by including the authorization code received in the previous step. When making the request, the client authenticates with the authorization server. The client includes the redirection URI used to obtain the authorization code for verification.

5.   The authorization server authenticates the client, validates the authorization code, and ensures that the redirection URI received matches the URI used to redirect the client in step 3. If valid, the authorization server responds back with an access token and, optionally, a refresh token.

Based on this description, we can highlight the characteristics explained in Figure 3-2.

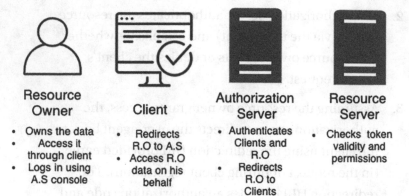

Figure 3-2. OAuth roles

The scenario described above is one example of how OAuth proposes that access granting should happen. The OAuth 2.0 specification, which is the current version, describes six different grant types:

- Authorization Code

- Client Credentials

- Device Code

- Refresh Token

- Implicit Flow

- Password Grant

Each grant type addresses different use cases. Our example uses the **Authorization Code** grant type, which is a better fit for web browser-based applications and mobile applications, where we usually want to authorize third-party sites or apps.

Besides defining roles and flows, the OAuth specification also defines client types, how to use tokens, a threat model, and security considerations that should be applied when implementing OAuth. My objective is not to fully discuss the specification, but to give you just enough information so you can understand what you are going to do later in this chapter.

OpenID Connect

OAuth is an authorization protocol, but to fully implement access control we also need definitions on how we work with authentication. In the words of the OpenID Foundation, "OpenID Connect 1.0 is a simple identity layer on top of the OAuth 2.0 protocol."[2] This is the protocol you are going to use when implementing access control.

There isn't much that I need you to know about OpenID Connect, besides that it is an identity layer on top of the OAuth 2.0. When we talk about grant types, we will be talking about the OAuth definition. When we talk about tokens, we will be talking about the JWT (JSON Web Tokens) implementation. So there isn't any specific concept from the OpenID Connect that I need you to understand in order to configure the IAM (Identity and Access Management) tool you will be using.

The OIDC specification is extensive. It goes from the core definition, which specifies authentication built on top of OAuth 2.0, to how to provide dynamic registration for clients, how to manage sessions, OpenID providers discovery, and so on. If you are curious about it and want to dive deeper into the subject, I recommend you visit the OpenID Foundation site, `https://openid.net/`. There you will find the complete specification as well as additional information about the protocol and how the community is evolving.

One side note, I would like to add that there was an OpenID specification before OpenID Connect. OpenID was the specification for authentication I mentioned when telling the history of OAuth's creation. The OpenID specification is now considered obsolete, so that is why it is common to hear OpenID when, in fact, people are referring to OpenID Connect, because OIDC replaced the first OpenID specification.

---

[2] This description was taken from the OpenID website, `https://openid.net/connect/`

Keycloak

We talked about protocols but now we need to start working with a solution that in fact implements them and offers other features that will combine with those protocols to offer a complete access control solution. This is Keycloak.

Besides the protocols that will allow us to have standards to follow and guarantee interoperability between our application and other solutions, there are other things that we need to worry about. Maybe the first one that comes to mind is, where and how am I going to persist/manage my user base? After all, how am I going to authenticate and authorize somebody if I don't have a list of users? That's why you are going to use Keycloak.

Keycloak implements two standards for authentication and authorization: **SAML 2.0** and **OpenID Connect**. As an identity management solution it provides a complete system for user management and the capacity to federate other user bases such as Kerberos or LDAP implementations. You could also implement a provider to adapt other user bases to it, as for example, a user base present in a SQL database. Another possibility is the brokering of another identity provider based on SAML 2.0 and OpenID Connect. This way you can have a single point for access control even working with different identity providers.

You will be only focusing on the OpenID Connect standard, but in case you want to know, SAML 2.0 is an XML-based standard built for the traditional web service world (SOAP), therefore it's a much older protocol. Just to give you an idea, the v2.0 version was released in 2005.

The best and fastest way to start experimenting with Keycloak is by using the container image provided by the project's community, and this is what you are going to do. From your terminal, run the following command:

```
$ docker run --name keycloak -e KEYCLOAK_USER=admin \
-e KEYCLOAK_PASSWORD=admin -p 8180:8080 -p 8543:8443 jboss/
keycloak:13.0.0
```

You are using Keycloak version 13.0.0, which is currently the latest one. You are setting the administrator user as admin and using admin for password. You are mapping its HTTP port to 8180 and its HTTPS port to 8543.

In your favorite web browser, visit http://localhost:8180. You should see a page like Figure 3-3.

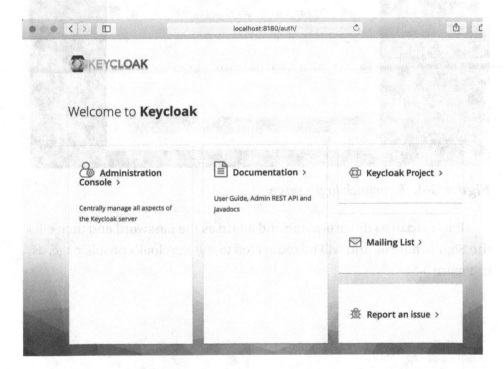

Figure 3-3. *Keycloak home page*

Click the Administration Console link. You will be redirected to the login page, as in Figure 3-4.

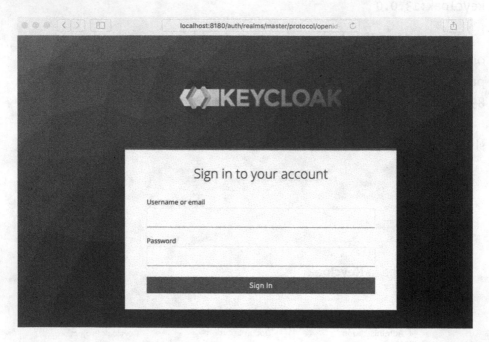

Figure 3-4.   Keycloak login page

Enter admin as the username and admin as the password and then click the Sign In button. You will be redirected to the Keycloak console page, as in Figure 3-5.

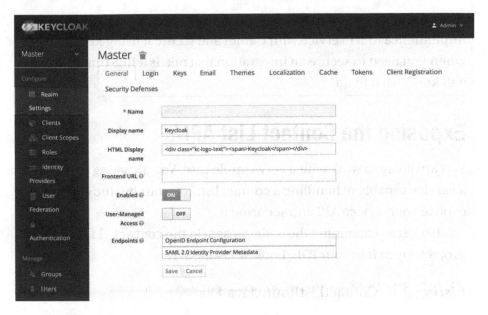

Figure 3-5. *Keycloak Administration Console*

You will stop with the Keycloak configuration at this point. You know how to run it and how to access it, but to start configuring Keycloak and start discussing its concepts, you need to see a use case for it.

Securing REST APIs with Keycloak

After discussing protocols and what Keycloak has to offer, your next step is to understand how to configure Camel applications to use Keycloak. First, you should analyze an example scenario.

True integration cases require at least two different applications or endpoints and one application to compose the integration layer. This may be a little bit too complex for example code. Since my objective is to teach you how to use Camel to solve common integration problems, I will follow an approach where you write more Camel code to solve different cases, even if that case is not necessarily an integration and you are actually implementing a service. This is what you are going to do now. You will implement a REST service with Camel and secure it using Keycloak. So when you need to secure an integration that needs a REST interface, you will know what to do.

Exposing the Contact List API

You are going to work with a very simple case. You are going to implement a service capable of handling a contact list. You start by studying how to expose your service API and securing it.

Let's start examining the code present in the `contact-list-api` project. Open it in your IDE. Look at Listing 3-1.

Listing 3-1.   ContactListRoute.java File

```java
public class ContactListRoute extends RouteBuilder {

public static final String MEDIA_TYPE_APP_JSON =
"application/json";

@Override
public void configure() throws Exception {
  rest("/contact")
  .bindingMode(RestBindingMode.json)
  .post()
    .consumes(MEDIA_TYPE_APP_JSON)
    .produces(MEDIA_TYPE_APP_JSON)
    .type(Contact.class)
    .route()
    .routeId("save-contact-route")
      .log("saving contacts")
      .bean("contactsBean", "addContact")
    .endRest()
```

```
.get()
.produces(MEDIA_TYPE_APP_JSON)
.route()
  .routeId("list-contact-route")
  .log("listing contacts")
  .bean("contactsBean", "listContacts")
.endRest();

    }
}
```

This service has only two operations: one to save a contact in the
list and one to list the contacts saved. The chosen media type is JSON,
something you already saw how to work with, but there is something new
for you to learn here: how to automatically convert the input and output
data of a REST interface.

By setting the bindingMode(RestBindingMode.json) you're telling
Camel that you want the incoming JSON data to be transformed into
a POJO object, in this case the type(Contact.class) for the post()
operation, and that the responses must be automatically converted to
JSON.

For this automatic binding you're using the camel-quarkus-jackson
data format, which is the default data format for the JSON REST binding
mode. This is why you don't need to declare a data format.

Besides the interface declaration, the magic really happens in
Listing 3-2. Take a look at it.

Listing 3-2. ContactBean.java File

```
@Singleton
@Unremovable
@Named("contactsBean")
public class ContactsBean {
```

```java
private Set<Contact> contacts = Collections.
newSetFromMap(Collections.synchronizedMap
(new LinkedHashMap<>()));
private static final Logger LOG = Logger.
getLogger(ContactsBean.class);

public ContactsBean() {}

@PostConstruct
public void init(){
contacts.add(new Contact("Bill","bill@email.com","99999999"));
contacts.add(new Contact("Joe", "joe@email.com","00000000"));
}

public void  listContacts(Message message) {
    message.setBody(contacts);
}

public void addContact(Message message) {
    if( message.getBody() != null){
        contacts.add(message.getBody(Contact.class)) ;
    }else{
        LOG.info("Empty body");
    }
}
}
```

The first thing to notice is that you're using the CDI specification to create a Singleton bean that carries a Linked Hash Map containing the list of contacts. You're also using the @PostConstruct to set some default entries to the hashmap after the bean is created. The listContacts() and addContact() methods are very straightforward, where addContact() takes the POJO from the body and puts it in the hashmap and listContacts() puts the hashmap into the message body to return the collection as the HTTP response.

The Contact POJO class is also very simple. Take a look at Listing 3-3.

Listing 3-3. Contact.java File

```java
public class Contact {

    public String name;
    public String email;
    public String phone;

    public Contact() {}

    public Contact(String name, String email, String phone) {
        this.name = name;
        this.email = email;
        this.phone = phone;
    }

    @Override
    public boolean equals(Object o) {
        if (this == o) return true;
        if (!(o instanceof Contact)) return false;
        Contact contact = (Contact) o;
        return Objects.equals(name, contact.name) && Objects.
        equals(email, contact.email) && Objects.equals(phone,
        contact.phone);
    }

    @Override
    public int hashCode() {
        return Objects.hash(name, email, phone);
    }
}
```

As you can see, there is no need for annotations in the POJO. Since this class has no special requirements, Jackson will know how to transform it to and from JSON. The only thing that is somewhat different is to implement the equals() and hashCode() methods. This is done to avoid duplicate entries in the contact list.

With that said, you can test the application. On your terminal, run the application using the Quarkus plugin:

```
contact-list-api $ mvn quarkus:dev
```

You can save a contact this way:

```
$ curl -X POST 'http://localhost:8080/contact' \
-H 'Content-Type: application/json' \
--data-raw '{ "phone": "333333333", "name": "Tester Tester",
"email": "tester@email.com"}'
```

And you can retrieve the list like this:

```
$ curl http://localhost:8080/contact
```

The service is working but is not protected. Before changing anything in the application, you must see how to properly configure Keycloak.

Configuring Keycloak

You saw how to run Keycloak locally. Now you will learn how to configure it and how to configure the applications.

You stopped the Keycloak introduction when you accessed the administrative console. Go back to the console. There are a few concepts that we must discuss first.

The first page you access after the login is the Realm Settings page. You can see that you are using the Master realm, its Display Name is Keycloak, and it exposes two endpoints: one for OpenID and one for SAML 2.0.

A realm is a collection of user bases and client applications that belong to the same domain. The Master realm represents the Keycloak server domain, from which other domains are originated. So let's create a realm for your use case. Follow these steps:

- On the upper left is the realm name with an arrow pointing down. Click the arrow.

- The Add realm button will appear. Click it.

- You will be redirected to the Realm Creation page. Enter `contact-list` as the name and click the Create button.

- At this point the realm is already created, but you can add additional information as the display name. Set it as `Contact List Hit` and press the Save button.

Now that you have the realm configured, you need to configure applications to use this realm. Applications are treated as clients by Keycloak. Follow these steps:

- On the left menu, click Clients.

- Now you are on the Client Listing page. As you can see, there are other clients already defined. These clients are the applications used by Keycloak to manage aspects of this realm. You don't need to worry about them now.

- Click the Create button.

- Enter `contact-list-api` as the Client ID. Leave the Client Protocol as openid-connect. Set the Root URL as `http://localhost:8080/contact`.

- Click the Save button.

After creating the client you will be redirected to the Client Settings page, shown in Figure 3-6.

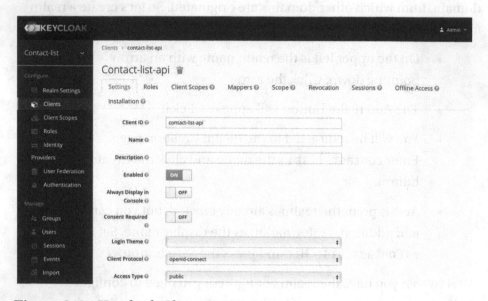

Figure 3-6. *Keycloak Client Settings page*

The only configuration left to do is to set the client Access Type to confidential. This way Keycloak will create a client and a secret for the client identification. Make the change and then, in the bottom of the page, press the Save button.

Once you have the realm and client configured, you need a user base that will be authenticated to consume the service. In this case, you are going to use Keycloak as your identity provider. Follow these steps to create users:

- On the left panel, click the Users menu. You will be redirected to the User Listing page.

- On the right side of the screen, click the Add user button.

- Set the username as viewer.

- Click the Save button. You will be redirected to the User Settings page, as in Figure 3-7.

Figure 3-7. *Keycloak User Settings page*

- Set the Email Verified attribute to **ON.**

- Now click the Credentials tab. Set the password as viewer. Make sure to set the Temporary attribute to *OFF*, as in Figure 3-8.

Figure 3-8. *Keycloak User Credentials page*

- Click the Set Password button. Now you have a user ready to test.

- Create another user called `editor` with the password of `editor` following the previous steps.

You now have a realm, clients, and users configured. The only thing left to configure are roles. You will adopt a role-based access control (RBAC) in your API, which means that you will need to assign roles to users. Based on those roles, the application will determine which actions a given user is authorized to do.

To create roles, use the following steps:

- On the left side panel, click the Roles menu option. It will get you to the Roles page, as in Figure 3-9.

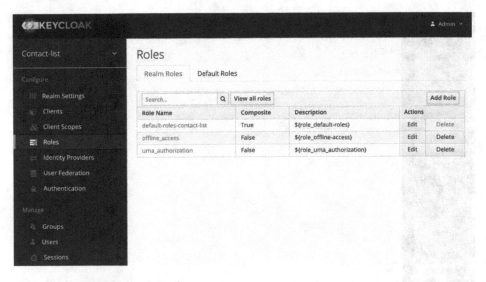

Figure 3 0. *Keycloak Roles page*

- You will create a role that is valid for the whole realm. Click the Add Role button on the right side of the screen.

- Set the Role Name as view. Keep the description blank and click the Save button.

- Do the same steps to create a role named edit.

With the roles created, you need to assign them to the users as described in the following steps:

- On the left panel menu, click Users.

- Click View all users. It will list the users created previously, as you can see in Figure 3-10.

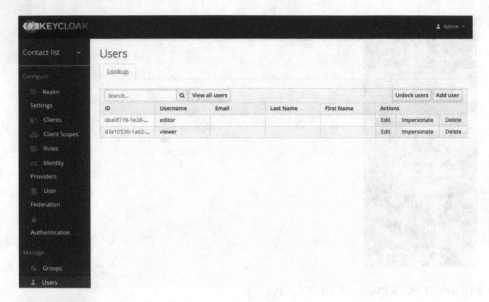

Figure 3-10. *Keycloak user list*

- Click the Edit button. This will lead you to the User Setting page.

- Click the Role Mappings tab. You will see the roles you created, like in Figure 3-11.

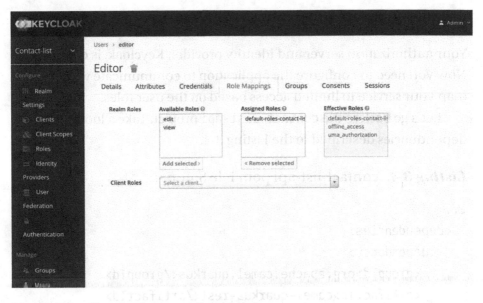

Figure 3-11. *Keycloak user role mappings*

- Since you are editing the `editor` user, click in the `edit` role.

- The Add selected button will be unblocked. Click it.

- You should receive the following message: "Success! Role mappings updated."

- Now edit the `viewer` user, adding the `view` role to it following the same steps.

Now you have your Keycloak configured for your application example. You also had the chance to get to know a little bit more about how it works and how to navigate its configurations.

Configuring The Resource Server

Your authorization server and identity provider, Keycloak, is configured. Now you need to configure the application to communicate with it and map your service to limited access based on the user roles.

Let's go back to the `contact-list-api` project. Take a look at the dependencies described in the Listing 3-4.

Listing 3-4. contact-list-api pom File Snippet

```
...
  <dependencies>
    <dependency>
      <groupId>org.apache.camel.quarkus</groupId>
      <artifactId>camel-quarkus-rest</artifactId>
    </dependency>
    <dependency>
      <groupId>org.apache.camel.quarkus</groupId>
      <artifactId>camel-quarkus-bean</artifactId>
    </dependency>
    <dependency>
      <groupId>org.apache.camel.quarkus</groupId>
      <artifactId>camel-quarkus-jackson</artifactId>
    </dependency>
<!--    <dependency>-->
<!--        <groupId>io.quarkus</groupId>-->
<!--<artifactId>quarkus-keycloak-authorization</artifactId>-->
<!--    </dependency>-->
  </dependencies>
...
```

There is one commented dependency, `quarkus-keycloak-authorization`. This extension provides a policy enforcer that enforces access to protected resources based on permissions. This is an addition

to your JAX-RS implementation by using Bearer Token Authentication
of tokens issued by OpenID Connect- and OAuth 2.0-compliant
authorization servers such as Keycloak. **Uncomment this dependency**.
Now take a look at Listing 3-5.

Listing 3-5. contact-list-api project, application.properties File

```
### Client Configuration
#quarkus.oidc.auth-server-url=http://localhost:8180/auth/
realms/contact-list
#quarkus.oidc.client-id=contact-list-api
#quarkus.oidc.credentials.secret=

### Path Policies Mapping
## only authenticated access will be allowed
#quarkus.http.auth.permission.authenticated.paths=/*
#quarkus.http.auth.permission.authenticated.
policy=authenticated
#
#quarkus.http.auth.policy.role-edit.roles-allowed=edit
#quarkus.http.auth.permission.edit.paths=/contact
#quarkus.http.auth.permission.edit.methods=POST
#quarkus.http.auth.permission.edit.policy=role-edit
#
#quarkus.http.auth.policy.role-view.roles-allowed=view,edit
#quarkus.http.auth.permission.view.paths=/contact
#quarkus.http.auth.permission.view.methods=GET
#quarkus.http.auth.permission.view.policy=role-view
```

The application was already ready to be protected by Keycloak. I only
commented the configuration so you could test the application without
having to configure Keycloak first. **Uncomment the properties**. Let's talk a
little bit about this configuration.

The first properties entries are related to how this application connects to the OIDC authorization server. This is why you have the Keycloak URL pointing to the realm you configured for this example. You also need information about the client, in this case the client id and its secret. You must have noticed that the secret property is blank. Since this value is generated automatically by Keycloak when you set the client as "confidential", you will have different results than mine.

Follow these steps to get your secret value:

- Log back into Keycloak.

- On the left panel menu, click Clients.

- Click the contact-list-api Client ID.

- On the Client Settings page, click the Credentials tab. You should see a page like Figure 3-12.

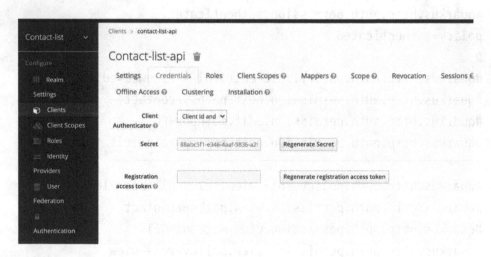

Figure 3-12. *Keycloak client credentials page*

- Copy the secret value in the grey input box and paste it in the blank `quarkus.oidc.credentials.secret` property.

The second part of the properties file is about how you map your protected resources and which policy you apply to them.

Take the `quarkus.http.auth.permission.authenticated.paths` property as an example. It uses a wildcard to mark every path to the policy pointed out in the `quarkus.http.auth.permission.authenticated.policy`, which is authenticated. This means that only requests with a valid bearer token will be accepted. Since this is a very generic rule, in the upcoming properties you describe more specific paths and combine them with HTTP methods to create a more granular access control. Observe the last part, shown in Listing 3-6.

Listing 3-6. Path Mapping in the application.properties File

```
...
quarkus.http.auth.policy.role-view.roles-allowed=view,edit
quarkus.http.auth.permission.view.paths=/contact
quarkus.http.auth.permission.view.methods=GET
quarkus.http.auth.permission.view.policy=role-view
...
```

Here you're creating a policy that authorizes any user with the roles view and edit and maps this policy to the /contact path and the GET HTTP method.

Let's start the application now and see what happens. Run the following command:

```
contact-list-api $ mvn quarkus:dev
```

Let's test it by listing the available contacts, but adding the -v switch to have more information in case of an error.

```
$ curl -v http://localhost:8080/contact
```

You will receive something similar to Figure 3-13.

```
~ $ curl -v http://localhost:8080/contact
*   Trying ::1...
* TCP_NODELAY set
* Connection failed
* connect to ::1 port 8080 failed: Connection refused
*   Trying 127.0.0.1...
* TCP_NODELAY set
* Connected to localhost (127.0.0.1) port 8080 (#0)
> GET /contact HTTP/1.1
> Host: localhost:8080
> User-Agent: curl/7.54.0
> Accept: */*
>
< HTTP/1.1 401 Unauthorized
< content-length: 0
<
* Connection #0 to host localhost left intact
```

Figure 3-13. *Unauthorized response*

Since you did not authenticate and didn't pass a valid token, you are not allowed to access this content, therefore you received a 401 HTTP code as a response.

In order to make this call successfully, first you need to get the client secret from the properties file (quarkus.oidc.credentials.secret) and set it as an environment variable like this:

$ export SECRET=[SECRET VALUE]

To get a valid token, run the following command:

$ curl -X POST http://localhost:8180/auth/realms/contact-list/
protocol/openid-connect/token \
--user contact-list-api:$SECRET \
    -H 'content-type: application/x-www-form-urlencoded' \
    -d 'username=viewer&password=viewer&grant_type=password'

There are a few things to break down in this command. The first thing is the URL you are accessing. It is the OpenID Connect token generation endpoint for your created realm. The second one is that you are using basic authentication to authenticate the client, using the client id as the username and the secret as the password. At last you have the user credentials and the grant type, which in this case is password. You are using the password grant here because this is not a web or mobile application where you could redirect the user to the authorization server. This is not even a process involving human interaction. So you need the application to know the user's credentials and there is no problem with that because you are in a single party application scenario.

After you run the command, you should receive something like Listing 3-7.

Listing 3-7. JSON Web Token Snippet

```
{
  "access_token": "eyJhbGciOiJSUzI1NiIsInR5cCIgOiA...",
  "expires_in": 300,
  "refresh_expires_in": 1800,
  "refresh_token": "eyJhbGciOiJIUzI1NiIsInR5w...",
  "token_type": "Bearer",
  "not-before-policy": 0,
  "session_state": "ff9a1588-863a-4745-9a28-87c8584b22cd",
  "scope": "email profile"
}
```

I cut the tokens represented here to make it fit better on the page. You can get a complete representation by using the provided command.

The response contains the token you need to get authorized but also other information about the token, such as its expiration, type, and scope. You also get a refresh token that allows the client to get new tokens and continue to access the resource server without a new authentication process.

Let's run a script to access the API. I'm using jq, a JSON command-line processor, to extract only the access token value. You may need to install the jq tool in your terminal. If you don't have access to it or another similar tool, you can extract this value manually and set it as the ACCESS_TOKEN variable, like in the following command:

```
$ export ACCESS_TOKEN=$( curl -s -X POST http://localhost:8180/
auth/realms/contact-list/protocol/openid-connect/token \
--user contact-list-api:$SECRET \
      -H 'content-type: application/x-www-form-urlencoded' \
      -d 'username=viewer&password=viewer&grant_type=password'
      | jq --raw-output '.access_token' )

$ curl -X GET http://localhost:8080/contact -H "Authorization:
Bearer $ACCESS_TOKEN"
```

You can try to add a new contact with the same token. Use the following command:

```
$ curl -X POST 'http://localhost:8080/contact' -H 'Content-
Type: application/json' \
-H "Authorization: Bearer $ACCESS_TOKEN" \
--data-raw '{"phone": "333333333","name": "Tester Tester",
"email": "tester@email.com"}'
```

It didn't work, right? This user is not authorized to make this call. Get yourself a valid token with the editor user like this:

```
$ export ACCESS_TOKEN=$( curl -s -X POST http://localhost:8180/
auth/realms/contact-list/protocol/openid-connect/token \
--user contact-list-api:cb4b7d21-e8f4-4223-9923-5cb98f00209a \
    -H 'content-type: application/x-www-form-urlencoded' \
    -d 'username=editor&password=editor&grant_type=password'
    | jq --raw-output '.access_token' )
```

You can try to insert the new contact now. After that, you can use the
GET method to list the contacts and see if the new one is there.

Consuming APIs with Camel

You have been creating REST APIs and testing them using the command
line, but you also need to learn how to consume APIs in your Camel
routes. In this example, you are going to learn how to do it, but also how to
consume APIs protected using OpenID Connect.

Start by loading the contact-list-client project in your favorite
IDE. Let's check the RouteBuilder first. See Listing 3-8.

Listing 3-8. OIDClientRoute.java File

```java
public class OIDClientRoute extends RouteBuilder {

    @Override
    public void configure() throws Exception {

        from("timer:OIDC-client-timer?period=3000")
            .routeId("OIDC-client-route")
            .bean("tokenHandlerBean")
            .to("vertx-http:http://localhost:8080/contact")
            .log("${body}");
    }
}
```

This is a simple route that will get the contact list from the API every three seconds. The only thing new here is that you are calling a web service using the vertx-http client.

Camel offers a good variety of HTTP clients to choose from. For this case I chose vertx-http for two main reasons: Vertx components have high performance and it is dependency compatible with the OIDC client used in this example.

Look at the dependencies declared in pom.xml in Listing 3-9.

Listing 3-9. contacts-list-client pom.xml Snippet

```
...
    <dependency>
      <groupId>org.apache.camel.quarkus</groupId>
      <artifactId>camel-quarkus-timer</artifactId>
    </dependency>
    <dependency>
      <groupId>org.apache.camel.quarkus</groupId>
      <artifactId>camel-quarkus-bean</artifactId>
    </dependency>
    <dependency>
      <groupId>io.quarkus</groupId>
      <artifactId>quarkus-oidc-client</artifactId>
    </dependency>
    <dependency>
      <groupId>org.apache.camel.quarkus</groupId>
      <artifactId>camel-quarkus-vertx-http</artifactId>
    </dependency>
...
```

You are already familiar with the camel-quarkus-timer and camel-quarkus-bean extensions. You have been using them throughout the examples. The new ones are quarkus-oidc-client and camel-quarkus-vertx-http. The HTTP client is responsible for sending the HTTP requests to your protected resource. The OIDC client is responsible for getting and managing your tokens.

Let's examine the bean responsible for dealing with the tokens in Listing 3-10.

Listing 3-10. TokenHandlerBean.java File

```java
@Singleton
@Unremovable
@Named("tokenHandlerBean")
public class TokenHandlerBean {

  @Inject
  OidcClient client;

  volatile Tokens currentTokens;

  @PostConstruct
  public void init() {
    currentTokens = client.getTokens().await().indefinitely();
  }

  public void insertToken(Message message){

    Tokens tokens = currentTokens;
    if (tokens.isAccessTokenExpired()) {
      tokens = client.refreshTokens(tokens.getRefreshToken())
.await().indefinitely();
      currentTokens = tokens;
    }

    message.setHeader("Authorization", "Bearer " + tokens.
    getAccessToken() );
  }
}
```

The main thing to notice is that you are injecting an `OidcClient` in this `Singleton` and after the bean is created you are getting a token from the authorization server. There is only a single method that can be bound for your route, the `insertToken()`. This method takes a message as an argument and checks if the current token is not expired. If it is, `insertToken()` will use the refresh token to generate a new valid access token and then pass its value to the message object as a header. You are passing it as a header because HTTP clients transform message headers into HTTP headers.

As you may imagine, the `OidcClient` configuration is done in the `application.properties` file. Take a look at Listing 3-11.

Listing 3-11. contact-list-client application.properties Snippet

```
...
quarkus.oidc-client.auth-server-url=http://localhost:8180/auth/
realms/contact-list/
quarkus.oidc-client.client-id=contact-list-client
quarkus.oidc-client.credentials.secret=
quarkus.oidc-client.grant.type=password
quarkus.oidc-client.grant-options.password.username=viewer
quarkus.oidc-client.grant-options.password.password=viewer
```

The configuration made here is very similar to what you did when testing the application using cURL. You continue to use password grant as your grant type, setting the same authentication server using the same user, but you need to use a different client, since this is a different application. As you may notice, the secret is blank so you need to create a client for this application in your Keycloak instance. Follow these steps in case you have forgotten how to do it:

- Log into the Keycloak console.

- On the left panel menu, click Clients.

- In the Client Listing page, click the Create button.

- Set the Client ID as contact-list-client. Set the Client Protocol as openid-connect. Don't set anything for the Root URL.

- Click the Save button.

- Set the Access Type as confidential and enter `http://localhost:8080` as the Valid Redirect URI.

- On the bottom of the page, click the Save button.

- Once the changes are saved, the Credentials tab will appear. Click it.

- Copy the secret value and past it in the project's `application.properties` file.

Your Client Listing page should look like Figure 3-14.

Client ID	Enabled	Base URL	Actions		
account	True	http://localhost:8180/auth/realms/contact-list/account/	Edit	Export	Delete
account-console	True	http://localhost:8180/auth/realms/contact-list/account/	Edit	Export	Delete
admin-cli	True	Not defined	Edit	Export	Delete
broker	True	Not defined	Edit	Export	Delete
contact-list-api	True	Not defined	Edit	Export	Delete
contact-list-client	True	Not defined	Edit	Export	Delete
realm-management	True	Not defined	Edit	Export	Delete
security-admin-console	True	http://localhost:8180/auth/admin/contact-list/console/	Edit	Export	Delete

Figure 3-14. *Client Listing page*

Now you are ready to test the two applications together. Open two terminal windows or tabs. In the first one, start the `contact-list-api` project. In the second one, start the `contact-list-client` project with the following command:

```
contact-list-client $ mvn clean quarkus:dev -Ddebug=5006
```

Since you are running both applications in debug mode, you need to change the debug port of the second one to avoid port conflicts.

At this point, you should start seeing log entries in the `contact-list-client` terminal showing the request results every three seconds. As you can see, clients that belong to the same realm can share user and role definitions, because in this case what matters is the authorization server they have in common, which is `http://localhost:8180/auth/realms/contact-list`.

There is another test you can do. With the two applications running, stop the Keycloak server. You will see that no error will appear. This happens because the resource server is validating the token by itself. Tokens are digitally signed and the client can check this signature to make sure the token is valid and wasn't tampered with. As long as the token is not expired, in our case the expiration time is 300 seconds (5 minutes), the client application will be able to access the resource server.

Of course, a lot more can be done with OIDC and Keycloak. We are just scratching the surface here. My idea was to introduce you to the protocols and to Keycloak and teach you how to deal with them in your Camel routes.

Summary

In this chapter, you learned about open standards regarding web application and services security, and implementing them using open source tools for IAM and for development. You learned the following:

- About the OAuth 2.0 protocol

- About the OpenID Connect protocol

- How to run and configure Keycloak

- How to protected Camel APIs with OIDC

- How to consume APIs using Camel

You will continue your journey by discussing persistence, as you learn more about Camel's concepts and integration patterns.

CHAPTER 4

Accessing Databases with Apache Camel

Most of what we do when implementing APIs or integrations is move data around. We provide data, consume it, transform it, replicate it, and so on. This way we enable front end systems or automated systems to do their tasks. In order to provide that capacity in our routes, at some point we will need to persist data or read data from a system specialized in persistence and data search. Usually it will involve databases.

There is a big and increasing variety of databases out there. We have the classical SQL and tabular databases, we have document-oriented databases, we have graph databases, and many more. Each of them is a fit for a specific use case, and for each use case there are different possibilities on how you can solve the problem. That is the line that I don't intend to cross in this chapter. Camel offers a great variety of components to access most types of databases. I can't cover all of them in this chapter. So here we will focus on relational databases because they have a more standardized access approach and are still one of the most common use cases.

From an integration standpoint, I want you to know how to access databases using Camel and the configurations you will need to do on Quarkus, so when a database integration case crosses your path, you will know how to access it using these tools. You will see mechanisms to maintain data consistency and how to deal with application exceptions.

As usual, as we discuss this chapter's main topics, we will engage in discussions regarding integration patterns. You'll also learn new Camel concepts.

Relational Databases

We start by looking at relational databases, which are the most commonly found database usage cases. You will see how to utilize the Java specification for database connectivity (JDBC) and Jakarta Persistence API (JPA) to interact with databases using Quarkus and Camel.

This book covers a lot of different technologies and use cases because Camel is a very broad and extensive tool. I want to give you a view of how Camel works and what its concepts are, but also give you practical examples of the most common use cases. Connecting to a relational database appears on the top 10 common use cases list.

Since we are talking about many different topics, the approach is always to go for the most common needs and features that showcase how that particular component works and why you should use it. I will give you a basic example, showing how to solve it. From that you may go forward with your studies and try to implement more complex use cases. This chapter will be no different.

I hope that you already have some familiarity with relational databases and especially how Java deals with them, but if you are a beginner in Java, do not worry. You will still be able to execute the examples presented in this book and understand what is being done.

Without further delay, let's see the examples.

Persistence with JPA

You need a use case to demonstrate how to use JDBC and JPA with Camel, so let's use one that you already know: the Contact List API. Let's replace the in-memory set of objects with an actual database.

Start by opening the contact-list-api-jpa project in your IDE. First, you have to analyze the extensions used in this example. Look at the pom. xml shown in Listing 4-1.

Listing 4-1. Project contact-list-api-jpa pom.xml Snippet

```
...
<dependencies>
  <dependency>
    <groupId>org.apache.camel.quarkus</groupId>
    <artifactId>camel-quarkus-rest</artifactId>
  </dependency>
  <dependency>
    <groupId>org.apache.camel.quarkus</groupId>
    <artifactId>camel-quarkus-jackson</artifactId>
  </dependency>
  <dependency>
    <groupId>org.apache.camel.quarkus</groupId>
    <artifactId>camel-quarkus-jpa</artifactId>
  </dependency>
  <dependency>
    <groupId>io.quarkus</groupId>
    <artifactId>quarkus-jdbc-h2</artifactId>
  </dependency>
</dependencies>
...
```

The first two dependencies you already know. You used camel-quarkus-rest to provide the REST DSL and camel-quarkus-jackson so you could have automatic binding for the incoming and outcoming JSON. The other three are the ones that will help you with the relational database connection.

119

You may have noticed that quarkus-jdbc-h2 has a different group id than the other dependencies. This library is not a Camel component, but a Quarkus extension to provide JDBC drivers for the given database and allow the configuration of data sources that will be used by the Camel component, in this case camel-quarkus-jpa. We will talk about it in a second.

Let's examine how the route changed. Look at Listing 4-2.

Listing 4-2. ContactListRoute.java File

```java
public class ContactListRoute extends RouteBuilder {

public static final String MEDIA_TYPE_APP_JSON = "application/
json";

@Override
public void configure() throws Exception {

  rest("/contact")
    .bindingMode(RestBindingMode.json)
   .post()
     .type(Contact.class)
     .outType(Contact.class)
     .consumes(MEDIA_TYPE_APP_JSON)
     .produces(MEDIA_TYPE_APP_JSON)
     .route()
        .routeId("save-contact-route")
        .log("saving contacts")
        .to("jpa:" + Contact.class.getName())
    .endRest()
  .get()
   .outType(List.class)
   .produces(MEDIA_TYPE_APP_JSON)
   .route()
```

```
        .routeId("list-contact-route")
        .log("listing contacts")
        .to("jpa:" + Contact.class.getName()+"?query={{query}}")
      .endRest();
}
}
```

This route is pretty much the same route you had in the previous chapter, but with some small changes to use a relational database to "persist" your data. I'm using the word persist between quotes because I'm not saving the data in a file and having that file saved in a durable storage unit. For this example, I'm using **H2** as an embedded in-memory database. This will allow you to run this example without having to configure a database instance in your machine, but you won't need to adapt anything to use it. Since this code uses JDBC and JPA, access to relational databases is standardized. So it doesn't really matter what relational database you are using, if it is JDBC compatible.

You need to use the extension (dependency) provided by the Quarkus project because of how Quarkus works. Using purely the JDBC driver provided by the database community or database provider may not work as expected.

Starting with how the contact is saved, in the post() operation the only thing that changed was the to("jpa:" + Contact.class.getName()) calling. Instead of calling a bean to save the POJO in an in-memory collection, what you're doing is calling the component provided by the camel-quarkus-jpa extension to save the POJO in the database. This component producer only requires the entity bean class name in order to ensure the correct body type. You are already sending the right type because you are using the JSON binding to transform the incoming JSON into the entity bean you need, the Contact class.

Take a look at how the Contact class is defined now. See Listing 4-3.

Listing 4-3. Contact.java File

```java
@Entity
public class Contact {

    @Id
    @GeneratedValue(strategy = GenerationType.IDENTITY)
    public Integer id;

    @Column(unique = true)
    public String name;
    public String email;
    public String phone;

    public Contact() { }
}
```

You can see some simplification in this class. There is no more overloaded constructor and no implementation for hash() or equals(). This class now represents a table in a relational database, therefore a did changes that will reflect relational tables characteristics. For example, a table needs a primary key, so I added a sequential numeral attribute that will be automatically generated when you insert a new row in that table and call it "id". The "id" attribute is annotated with @Id to indicate that this is the primary key and with @GeneratedValue, so every new entry without the id value will get an id value produced by an identity column in the database.

Look now at the application.properties file in Listing 4-4 and check how you are defining the access to the database.

Listing 4-4. contact-list-api-jpa application.properties

```
# datasource configuration
quarkus.datasource.db-kind = h2
quarkus.datasource.username = h2
quarkus.datasource.password = h2
quarkus.datasource.jdbc.url = jdbc:h2:mem:db;DB_CLOSE_DELAY=-1

# drop and create the database at startup
quarkus.hibernate-orm.database.generation=drop-and-create

query=select c from Contact c
```

Most of the application configuration in Quarkus is done by just setting values in the application.properties file and with data sources it is no different. You only need to set the parameters and Quarkus will create the connection factory for you. Let's analyze these parameters.

You start by setting quarkus.datasource.db-kind with the database you are going to use, in your case H2.

Currently, besides H2, the following options are available in Quarkus:

- Apache Derby

- IBM DB2

- MariaDB

- Microsoft SQL Server

- MySQL

- Oracle Database

- PostgreSQL

The username and password are generic values. Since you are using the embedded mode, you are creating the database during the application startup using the provided information, so any value can be used.

The `quarkus.datasource.jdbc.url` has more information about what should be created. By setting `mem:db` you're saying to H2 that you want to create an in-memory database called `db`. You want that database to be available in the JVM for as long as the JVM exists, that is why `DB_CLOSE_DELAY` is a negative number. The remaining configurations are related to schema creation and the JPQL query you will use for searching. The JPA component leverages Hibernate as the JPA implementation and you use Quarkus Hibernate configuration properties to set Hibernate as you need. In this example, you are telling Hibernate that you want to recreate your database schema every time you start the application. This makes a lot of sense because the database itself is recreated every time the application starts.

The search logic or the GET operation didn't change much either, but now you call the JPA component to perform a JPQL query for you. There is something new in the call `to("jpa:"+Contact.class.getName()+"?query={{query}}")`. The value between the double braces is taken from the properties file. By using double braces you can access values in the properties file and change how you declare the elements in the routes. In this example, you only set a parameter, but you could have done more.

In a future topic, we will dive deeper in how we can use properties to write Camel routes. For now, we continue to discuss access to relational databases.

With the query "`select c from Contact c`" you return every entry in the Contact table and since you are using an ORM, the result will be a `List.class` of `Contact.class`. This return will be automatically converted to JSON for the HTTP response.

Let's try this application. Run it with the following command on your terminal:

```
contact-list-api-jpa $ mvn quarkus:dev
```

You can start by searching for contact entries. You know that there is nothing there, but you want to check how the application is behaving. You can make the following request:

```
$ curl -v -w '\n' http://localhost:8080/contact
```

Use the switch -v so you know what the HTTP response code is. The response you got should be something similar to Figure 4-1.

```
~ $ curl -v -w '\n' http://localhost:8080/contact
*    Trying ::1...
* TCP_NODELAY set
* Connection failed
* connect to ::1 port 8080 failed: Connection refused
*    Trying 127.0.0.1...
* TCP_NODELAY set
* Connected to localhost (127.0.0.1) port 8080 (#0)
> GET /contact HTTP/1.1
> Host: localhost:8080
> User-Agent: curl/7.54.0
> Accept: */*
>
< HTTP/1.1 200 OK
< Content-Length: 2
< Content-Type: application/json
<
* Connection #0 to host localhost left intact
[]
```

Figure 4-1. *GET operation response*

As you can see, you got a successful response from the API. Since you don't have any entries yet, you got an empty list as a response. This may be an unwanted behavior, though. When you don't have entries, you may want to respond with a 204 HTTP code, which means "no content found." In this case, you need to add validation logic after the JPA component response, since it will return a list always.

Now let's add an entry to the database using the API. Run the following command in your terminal:

```
$ curl -w '\n' -X POST 'http://localhost:8080/contact' \
-H 'Content-Type: application/json' \
--data-raw '{ "phone": "333333333", "name": "Tester Tester", "email": "tester@email.com"}'
```

You should receive a response similar to Listing 4-5.

Listing 4-5. POST Operation Response

```
{
  "id": 1,
  "name": "Tester Tester",
  "email": "tester@email.com",
  "phone": "333333333"
}
```

You didn't send an id, but since your entry was persisted, a new id was generated for it. In this case, the response of the JPA component was the persisted object in the database.

Let's add two more entries before searching for them. Run the following commands in your terminal:

```
$ curl -X POST 'http://localhost:8080/contact' \
-H 'Content-Type: application/json' \
--data-raw '{ "phone": "1111111", "name": "Jane Doe", "email": "jane.d@email.com"}'
```

```
$ curl -X POST 'http://localhost:8080/contact' \
-H 'Content-Type: application/json' \
--data-raw '{ "phone": "2222222", "name": "John Doe", "email":
"john.d@email.com"}'
```

Now you can search for the contacts with the following command:

```
$ curl http://localhost:8080/contact
```

If you only added these three contacts, your response should be like Listing 4-6.

Listing 4-6. GET Operation Response

```
[{
  "id": 1,
  "name": "Tester Tester",
  "email": "tester@email.com",
  "phone": "333333333"
}, {
  "id": 2,
  "name": "Jane Doe",
  "email": "jane.d@email.com",
  "phone": "1111111"
}, {
  "id": 3,
  "name": "John Doe",
  "email": "john.d@email.com",
  "phone": "2222222"
}]
```

Parameterized Queries with JPA

In the first example using the JPA component, you did a simple find all query, but commonly you need to parameterize queries to retrieve only the specific entries in the database. Now you will learn how to make different searches using the JPA component and how to pass parameters values dynamically to queries.

In order to learn more about how the JPA component works, you need to make a few changes to the contact-list-api-jpa project. Instead of applying changes on top of it, let's work with a new project: the contact-list-api-v2.

Open it in your IDE. Let's start by analyzing the RouteBuilder; see Listing 4-7.

Listing 4-7. ContactListRoute.java Snippet

```
public class ContactListRoute extends RouteBuilder {

    public static final String MEDIA_TYPE_APP_JSON =
    "application/json";

    @Override
    public void configure() throws Exception {

        declareInterface();
        declareGetListContactRoute();
        declareSearchContactByIdRoute();
        declareSaveContactRoute();

    }

    private void declareInterface(){
        rest("/contact")
        .bindingMode(RestBindingMode.json)
        .post()
```

```
        .type(Contact.class)
        .outType(Contact.class)
        .consumes(MEDIA_TYPE_APP_JSON)
        .produces(MEDIA_TYPE_APP_JSON)
        .to("direct:create-contact")
    .get()
        .outType(List.class)
        .produces(MEDIA_TYPE_APP_JSON)
        .to("direct:list-contacts")
    .get("/{id}")
        .outType(Contact.class)
        .produces(MEDIA_TYPE_APP_JSON)
        .to("direct:search-by-id");
}
```

...

I decided to change how I was declaring the route because now the route starts to become a little more complex. Instead of declaring the route logic nested in the REST DSL, I decided to separate each route and call them using direct. This way I can improve code readability and it will be easier to explain things by small parts.

The declareInterface() method is responsible for declaring the REST API interface. Notice the new GET operation, but this one is using a path parameter. The idea is that you will always retrieve a single result for this case, which is why you change the outType() to Contact.class instead of List.class.

Let's start with the search by id. Look at how the route is implemented in Listing 4-8.

Listing 4-8. declareSearchByContactId Method

```
private void declareSearchContactByIdRoute(){
from("direct:search-by-id")
  .routeId("search-by-id-route")
  .log("Searching Contact by id = ${header.id}")
  .setBody(header("id").convertTo(Integer.class))

  .to("jpa:" + Contact.class.getName()+ "?findEntity=true");
}
```

Here you are using a new query parameter in the JPA component declaration, findEntity. When findEntity is set to true, the component will attempt to find a single instance of the class declared in the component URI path parameter, in this case Contact.class.getName(). The component will use the message body as the key for the select operation. This is why you need the header() fluent builder. Since the key for the Contact class is an Integer object, the fluent builder is extracting the value passed as a URL parameter from the header, parsing it as an Integer object, and setting it in the message body.

Let's try this part of the code. You won't need to send a few post requests to have something to search for. Take a look at the import.sql file in the resources directory (Listing 4-9).

Listing 4-9. import.sql File

```
INSERT INTO CONTACT(NAME,EMAIL,PHONE,COMPANY) VALUES
('John Doe','john.d@email.com','1111111','MyCompany');
INSERT INTO CONTACT(NAME,EMAIL,PHONE,COMPANY) VALUES
('Jane Doe','jane.d@email.com','2222222','MyCompany');
INSERT INTO CONTACT(NAME,EMAIL,PHONE,COMPANY) VALUES
('Tester Test','test@email.com','00000000','Another Company');
```

This file is used to execute DML commands after Hibernate creates the schema. This way you can run a couple of insert commands to populate the database before you start testing. You still may use the POST operation if you want to add more entries, but now you don't need to do it to test searches.

Start the application and run the following command in your terminal:

```
contact-list-api-v2 $ mvn quarkus:dev
```

You can start searching by id like this:

```
$ curl -w '\n' http://localhost:8080/contact/2
```

The result should look like Figure 4-2.

```
~ $ curl -w '\n' http://localhost:8080/contact/2
{"id":2,"name":"Jane Doe","email":"jane.d@email.com",
"phone":"2222222","company":"MyCompany"}
```

Figure 4-2. *Search by Id response*

Now, let's take a look at how the list search route looks; see Listing 4-10.

Listing 4-10. declareGetListContactRoute Method

```
private void declareGetListContactRoute(){
 from("direct:list-contacts")
 .routeId("list-contact-route")
 .choice()
 .when(simple("${header.company} != null"))
  .log("Listing contacts by company = ${header.company}")
  .to("jpa:" + Contact.class.getName()+ "?query={{query.company
  }}&parameters=#mapParameters")
 .otherwise()
  .to("jpa:"+Contact.class.getName()+"?query={{query.all}}");
}
```

Now the list contacts route will be able to do two different searches, retrieve all the contacts, or find the contacts of a given company. As you may have noticed in the insert statements, a new field was added to the Contact entity, the company. This field represents something in common for contacts in a contact list and helps to exemplify how searches with a specific and dynamic parameter work.

You had to use a conditional flow with choice because both searches have the same path and method. The only difference is that when you want to search based on a company, you must pass the company's name as a query parameter in the HTTP request. So you check if the header.company is null, and if it is not, you search based on the company's name. Otherwise you retrieve all entries. If you look at the query.company property value, you will see that now you are using the "where" clause in your JPQL query. See Listing 4-11.

Listing 4-11. application.properties File Snippet

```
...
query.all=select c from Contact c
query.company=select c from Contact c where c.company =
:company
```

The query uses a named parameter, :company, as the condition of the where clause. If you go back to the route and look at the JPA component declaration, besides the query, you are also passing a bean reference as a parameter with "parameters=#mapParameters". This query parameter expects a reference of a Map<String,Object> object. Look at the last method in the class shown in Listing 4-12.

Listing 4-12. createMapParameters Method

```
@Produces()
@Named("mapParameters")
public Map createMapParameters(){
  Map<String, Object> parameters = new HashMap<>();
  parameters.put("company", "${header.company}" );
  return  parameters; }
```

You are using CDI to register a named bean containing the parameters you need for that query. You use the JPQL named parameter as the key for the map and you can set any object as the value. In this case, you are using a Simple expression to dynamically retrieve the value from the message header for each exchange. Since the header return value will be a String object, you don't need to worry about object parsing.

Let's try these operations. With the application running, execute the following command to return all the entries:

```
$ curl http://localhost:8080/contact
```

To search based on a company's name, you can use the following command:

```
$ curl http://localhost:8080/contact?company=Another%20Company
```

In this example, only a single result will be returned, as you can see in Figure 4-3, because you only have one entry where the company's name is equal to "Another Company."

```
~ $ curl -w '\n' http://localhost:8080/contact?company=Another%20Company
[{"id":3,"name":"Tester Test","email":"test@email.com","phone":"00000000
","company":"Another Company"}]
```

Figure 4-3. *Search by Company's name response*

You could also pass parameters in a more dynamic way using headers. Listing 4-13 shows the route.

133

Listing 4-13. Alternative Way to Pass Parameters

```
private void declareGetListContactRoute(){
from("direct:list-contacts")
.routeId("list-contact-route")
.choice()
.when(simple("${header.company} != null"))
.log("Listing contacts by company = ${header.company}")
.process(new Processor() {
  @Override
  public void process(Exchange exchange) throws Exception {
    Map<String, Object> parameters = new HashMap<>();
    parameters.put("company", "${header.company}" );
    exchange.getMessage().setHeader(
        JpaConstants.JPA_PARAMETERS_HEADER, parameters);
  }
})
.to("jpa:"+Contact.class.getName()+"?query={{query.company}}")
.otherwise()
.to("jpa:"+Contact.class.getName()+"?query={{query.all}}");
}
```

As you can see, in this example you won't need to pass a bean reference as a query parameter in the component configuration. You are sending the parameters dynamically using the JPA_PARAMETERS_HEADER header.

Particularly for this example, the first approach is better because you are not really changing the parameter value since you are using Simple. Here you have a reference for when you need to use a different object type that still needs to be passed dynamically.

Transactions

One very important concern when dealing with databases is how to keep
the data in a consistent state. Of course the databases already implement
many mechanisms to guarantee data consistency, but the database cannot
control if the application accessing it is performing the correct operations
to change the database state. By correct operations I mean changing the
database state and keeping it consistent with the systems or applications
using it.

When you are developing routes, most times you will be connecting
at least two different endpoints. In the previous example, you used a
REST interface with a database and you used Camel to implement a
REST service persisted in a database. Although this is a totally functional
implementation, this is not an integration. You were just using Camel to
implement a service.

Let's put the persistence needs in an integration scenario. Look at
Figure 4-4.

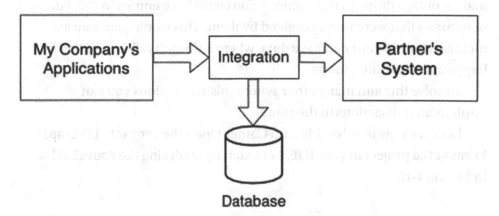

Figure 4-4. *Persisting data during integration*

Imagine that you work in a company that has applications that need to access a specific system provided by a partner. Instead of accessing the system directly, it was decided by the architecture team that the applications should consume this service through an integration layer and that layer, besides other things, should audit what was sent to the partner system by persisting the request in a database.

In a roughly and over simplistic representation, the route could look like Listing 4-14.

Listing 4-14. Model Route

```
from("{{rest.interface.definition}}")
.to("{{database.component.definition}}")
.to("{{partner.system.endpoint}}");
```

In an ideal world, this would work every time, but the world is never what we expect it to be, is it? What would happen if the partner's system had an outage during a transaction? You could have entries in the database of requests that were never received by them. This would generate an inconsistency in your database data, where it doesn't reflect what really happened in the integration.

To solve this and many other synchronism situations you can implement transactions in the route.

Let's see how to solve this with Camel. Open the contact-list-api-transacted project in your IDE. Let's start by analyzing the RouteBuilder in Listing 4-15.

Listing 4-15. ContactListRoute.java Snippet

```java
public class ContactListRoute extends RouteBuilder {

@Override
public void configure() throws Exception {
rest("/contact")
.bindingMode(RestBindingMode.json)
.post()
  .type(Contact.class)
  .outType(Contact.class)
  .consumes(APP_JSON)
  .produces(APP_JSON)
  .route()
    .routeId("save-contact-route")
    .transacted()
    .log("saving contacts")
    .to("jpa:" + Contact.class.getName())
    .log("Pausing the Transaction")
    .process(new Processor() {
    @Override
    public void process(Exchange exchange) throws Exception {
        Thread.sleep(7000);
    }
    })
    .log("Transaction Finished")
  .endRest()
.get()
  .outType(List.class)
  .produces(APP_JSON)
  .route()
```

```
    .routeId("list-contact-route")
  .to("jpa:"+Contact.class.getName()+ "?query={{query.all}}");
}
}
```

I made some changes for this example. I simplified the search, so
there's only a search all now. I also removed the import.sql, since we
won't need any entry in the database for the test, but the main change is
on the save contact route. The transacted() invocation indicates that we
want these route exchange executions to be transacted, which means the
operation in the route will only be committed when the exchange is done.

Transaction behavior depends on the components being used. Not all
of them really support transactions. They have to be able to perform
late commits and rollback operations in case of failure, something
that is not possible for HTTP clients, for example. In this case, we are
using the JPA component that is transaction compatible and will join
the transaction automatically.

To make this work, another configuration was required. Look at the
pom.xml, shown in Listing 4-16.

Listing 4-16. pom.xml File Dependencies Snippet

```
...
<dependencies>
    <dependency>
        <groupId>org.apache.camel.quarkus</groupId>
        <artifactId>camel-quarkus-rest</artifactId>
    </dependency>
    <dependency>
        <groupId>org.apache.camel.quarkus</groupId>
```

```
    <artifactId>camel-quarkus-jackson</artifactId>
  </dependency>
  <dependency>
    <groupId>org.apache.camel.quarkus</groupId>
    <artifactId>camel-quarkus-jpa</artifactId>
  </dependency>
  <dependency>
    <groupId>io.quarkus</groupId>
    <artifactId>quarkus-jdbc-h2</artifactId>
  </dependency>
  <dependency>
    <groupId>org.apache.camel.quarkus</groupId>
    <artifactId>camel-quarkus-jta</artifactId>
  </dependency>
</dependencies>
```

If you look at the dependencies of camel-quarkus-jpa you will see quarkus-hibernate-orm. As I said earlier, Hibernate is Quarkus' chosen JPA implementation. This extension uses quarkus-narayana for the JTA (Jakarta Transaction API) implementation. So to make this transaction manager available to Camel, you need the camel-quarkus-jta extension. It enables Camel to use Narayana transaction manager as transaction policies.

Let's try this code. Open three terminal windows or tabs. One of them you will use to run the application. The second one you will use to send a POST request to save an entity in the database and in the third you will get the data persisted in the database.

In the first window or tab, run the following command:

```
contact-list-api-transacted $ mvn quarkus:dev
```

Once the application has started, you can send a POST like this:

```
$ curl -X POST 'http://localhost:8080/contact' -H 'Content-
Type: application/json' --data-raw '{ "phone": "2222222",
"name": "John Doe", "email": "john.d@email.com"}'
```

There's a seven seconds thread sleep after the JPA invocation is done. This will demonstrate that even though you have already "processed" the change, the data wasn't persisted in the database because the transaction wasn't committed.

In the third window you may list the contacts like this:

```
$ curl http://localhost:8080/contact
```

You will see that during the seven seconds window cURL will only return an empty list, but once the seven seconds have passed you'll see "Transaction Finished" in the application logs and the GET request will return the entity you sent in the POST command.

One important thing to have in mind when configuring transactions is how you are defining your transaction boundaries. By boundaries I mean where your transaction should start and where it should finish. This can be done by setting the appropriate propagation behavior for the transaction.

There are six propagation policies to choose from. They are

- PROPAGATION_REQUIRED: It is the default option. Starts a transaction if none was started or stays with the existing one.

- PROPAGATION_REQUIRES_NEW: It starts a transaction if none was started. If there is one started, it suspends it and starts a new one.

- PROPAGATION_MANDATORY: It launches an exception if no transaction was started.

- PROPAGATION_SUPPORTS: If there is a transaction, it joins it; otherwise, it works with no transaction.

- PROPAGATION_NOT_SUPPORTED: If there is a transaction, it will be suspended for that boundary and this process part will work with no transaction.

- PROPAGATION_NEVER: It launches an exception if there is a transaction. It works without a transaction.

In the examples we will be using the default option as it is the most common case.

The first example intends to show how the commit process works, but another very important capacity of transactions is to roll back operations in case of failure. Let's test this. Perform the change in Listing 4-17 in the ContactListRoute.java in the contact-list-api-transacted project, where instead of using thread sleep you will throw an exception.

Listing 4-17. ContactListRoute.java Changes

```
...
.process(new Processor() {
    @Override
    public void process(Exchange exchange) throws Exception {
        throw new Exception("Testing Rollback Exception.")
    }
})
...
```

Run the application again if you have stopped it. Try to make another POST request. You will receive an error, a HTML response page with a stack trace in it. If you try to list all the contacts, you will receive an empty list as a response.

The transaction prevents you from putting the database in an inconsistent state. The operation wasn't over, so you couldn't have that register in the database.

Now remove the `transacted()` call. You may comment the line like this: `//.transacted()`

Do the same test. You will still receive an error message as a response, but now you have an entry in your database that shouldn't be there.

To work properly with transactions, you also need to specify ways to handle failures. So far I have been coding in an optimistic way, where I don't consider that certain operations may fail during execution. Obviously the intention here is to keep the code simple and easy to understand, but also I want to talk specifically of the different ways Camel provides exception handling. We dive into this next.

Handling Exceptions

To expect that exceptions may occur and to prepare for them is a very important programming good practice, and even more when we are talking about integration. We cannot really trust what is on the other side, even if it's an application that we code ourselves. Networks are not always reliable, applications may crash, and hardware can fail, so we need to prepare our application to handle exceptions to avoid losing data or leave the system in an inconsistent state. Next, you are going to see different ways to handle exceptions with Camel.s

Try-Catch-Finally

Similar to what we do when handling exceptions using Java, Camel also has `try/catch/finally` clauses that can be used in the route declaration. Let's see some examples on how to do it.

Start by opening the camel-try-catch project in your IDE. Let's analyze the TryCatchRoute.java file shown in Listing 4-18.

Listing 4-18. TryCatchRoute.java Snippet

```
public void configure() throws Exception {
rest("/tryCatch")
.bindingMode(RestBindingMode.json)
.post()
.type(Fruit.class)
.outType(String.class)
.consumes(APP_JSON)
.produces(TEXT_PLAIN)
.route()
 .routeId("taste-fruit-route")
 .doTry()
   .choice()
   .when(simple("${body.name} == 'apple' "))
     .throwException(new Exception("I don't like this fruit"))
   .otherwise()
     .setBody(constant("I like this fruit!"))
 .endDoTry()
 .doCatch(Exception.class)
   .setHeader(Exchange.HTTP_RESPONSE_CODE, constant(500))
   .setBody(exceptionMessage())
 .doFinally()
   .setHeader(Exchange.CONTENT_TYPE,constant(TEXT_PLAIN))
   .log("Exchange processing completed!")
.endRest();
}
```

This route has a simple logic to demonstrate how try/catch/finally works with Camel. This REST API has a single operation that receives a Fruit.class object as JSON and validates if the fruit name is "apple". If it is "apple", it throws an exception saying "I don't like this fruit"; otherwise, it responds with a simple phrase, "I like this fruit!". That's why I called this route "taste-fruit-route". By the way, I do like apples: this is just an example.

One thing that is new here is how you are using the Simple language to execute a method. By setting "${body.name}" you know that the object in the body has a method called name and the return is an object that you can compare with the string "apple". Let's look at the Fruit.java file in Listing 4-19.

Listing 4-19. Fruit.java File

```
@Entity
public class Fruit {

  @Id
  @GeneratedValue(strategy = GenerationType.IDENTITY)
  private Integer id;

  @Column(unique = true)
  private String name;

  public String getName() {
      return name;
  }

  public void setName(String name) {
      this.name = name;
  }

  public Integer getId() {
      return id;
  }
```

```
public void setId(Integer id) {
    this.id = id;
}
}
```

In the previous examples, I used the public access modifier for the class attributes to keep the code smaller, but for this example I needed a method to make the Simple expression work, which is why I chose to use getters and setters.

In order to make method invocation using Simple, you will need to add the camel-quarkus-bean extension to your project.

Once the condition is met, an exception is thrown using the DSL throwException(). This exception will be caught by your doCatch() clause, which will treat the exception by setting the right response headers and an appropriate message to the client. The doFinally() clause will be executed independently if an exception is thrown, so you use it to set the right Content-Type for the response and log that the exchange processing was completed.

The exceptionMessage() invocation is a value builder that encapsulates a Simple expression like this: "${exception.message}".

Let's test this route. Open a terminal and run the application:

```
camel-try-catch$ mvn quarkus:dev
```

You can send a request like this:

```
$ curl -w '\n' -X POST http://localhost:8080/tryCatch \
-H 'Content-Type: application/json' -d '{"name":"grape"}'
```

Since this is not an apple, you won't fall in the exception, as shown in Figure 4-5.

```
~ $ curl -w '\n' -X POST http://localhost:8080/tryCatch \
> -H 'Content-Type: application/json' -d '{"name":"grape"}'
I like this fruit!
```

Figure 4-5. *TryCatch route response*

Try a request that will cause the exception to be thrown:

```
$ curl -w '\n' -X POST http://localhost:8080/tryCatch \
-H 'Content-Type: application/json' -d '{"name":"apple"}'
```

You will get an answer like Figure 4-6.

```
~ $ curl -w '\n' -X POST http://localhost:8080/tryCatch \
> -H 'Content-Type: application/json' -d '{"name":"apple"}'
I don't like this fruit
```

Figure 4-6. *An exception is thrown.*

As you can see, try/catch/finally works in a very similar way as in the Java language. You could have multiple doCatch() clauses, you could nest a try/catch/finally inside a doTry(), and so on.

Let's see how a transacted route with try/catch looks. In the same project as before, open the TryCatchTransactedRoute.java file, shown in Listing 4-20.

Listing 4-20. TryCatchTransactedRoute.java

```java
public class TryCatchTransactedRoute extends RouteBuilder {

@Override
public void configure() throws Exception {
rest("/tryCatchTransacted")
  .bindingMode(RestBindingMode.json)
  .post()
    .type(Fruit.class)
    .outType(String.class)
    .consumes(APP_JSON)
    .produces(TEXT_PLAIN)
    .route()
      .transacted()
      .routeId("save-fruit-route")
      .doTry()
      .to("jpa:" + Fruit.class.getName())
      .choice()
      .when(simple("${body.name} == 'apple' "))
      .throwException(new Exception("I don't like this fruit"))
        .otherwise()
        .setHeader(Exchange.CONTENT_TYPE,constant(TEXT_PLAIN))
        .setBody(constant("I like this fruit!"))
      .endDoTry()
      .doCatch(Exception.class)
        .setHeader(Exchange.HTTP_RESPONSE_CODE,constant(500))
        .setHeader(Exchange.CONTENT_TYPE,constant(TEXT_PLAIN))
        .setBody(exceptionMessage())
        .markRollbackOnly()
    .endRest()
  .get()
```

```
    .outType(List.class)
    .produces(APP_JSON)
    .route()
     .routeId("list-fruits")
     .to("jpa:"+Fruit.class.getName()+"?query={{query.all}}");
  }
}
```

This route is different from the previous one. Instead of just analyzing the fruit name, it will also save a fruit in the database. Fruit names must have a unique value, as you saw in the Fruit class declaration, and if you try to save a fruit with a repeated name, a constraint violation exception will be thrown. This route also has a GET operation to allow you to retrieve a fruit list from the database.

One thing that you may have noticed is that there is no doFinally() clause. This happens because of the way you must deal with the rollback of transactions. If you analyze the doCatch() block, the last step is markRollbackOnly(). This means you are going to roll back the transaction at this point, but without throwing an exception, which means that the exception was handled properly. After this point, nothing gets executed, which is why you prepare the response, by setting the headers and the body, before the call. That is also the reason why you didn't use doFinally() here. It would only be executed if no exceptions happened.

Test this route. With the application running, run this command twice:

```
$ curl -X POST http://localhost:8080/tryCatchTransacted \
-H 'Content-Type: application/json' -d '{"name":"pineapple"}'
-w '\n' -v
```

On your second request you will receive something similar to Figure 4-7.

```
~ $ curl -X POST http://localhost:8080/tryCatchTransacted \
> -H 'Content-Type: application/json' -d '{"name":"pineapple"}' -w '\n' -v
Note: Unnecessary use of -X or --request, POST is already inferred.
*   Trying ::1...
* TCP_NODELAY set
* Connection failed
* connect to ::1 port 8080 failed: Connection refused
*   Trying 127.0.0.1...
* TCP_NODELAY set
* Connected to localhost (127.0.0.1) port 8080 (#0)
> POST /tryCatchTransacted HTTP/1.1
> Host: localhost:8080
> User-Agent: curl/7.54.0
> Accept: */*
> Content-Type: application/json
> Content-Length: 20
>
* upload completely sent off: 20 out of 20 bytes
< HTTP/1.1 500 Internal Server Error
< Accept: */*
< User-Agent: curl/7.54.0
< transfer-encoding: chunked
< Content-Type: text/plain
<
* Connection #0 to host localhost left intact
org.hibernate.exception.ConstraintViolationException: could not execute statement
```

Figure 4-7. *TryCatchTransacted route response*

The content type and HTTP status code are exactly what you set in the
doCatch() block and the response body is the exception message.

Now try to send "apple" as the request:

```
$ curl -X POST http://localhost:8080/tryCatchTransacted \
-H 'Content-Type: application/json' -d '{"name":"apple"}'
```

Then check if there is any "apple" in the database:

```
$ curl http://localhost:8080/tryCatchTransacted
```

Using transacted plus try/catch allows you to capture exceptions,
provide a treated response to your client, and roll back actions that would
make your database inconsistent, but this is not the only way to do it. Let's
learn a new one.

Error Handlers

The use of try/catch/finally is an easy way to handle localized exceptions, where you are capturing exceptions of a given block inside the route. I decided to start with them because they are similar to what we have in the Java language, but there are other ways to handle exceptions that go beyond a mapped block in the route. Let's see them.

Camel comes with predefined strategies to handle exceptions called error handlers. There are four error handlers and they are separated into two categories, transacted and non-transacted.

The non-transacted are

- DefaultErrorHandler: It is the default error handler. It will propagate exceptions back to the callers.

- DeadLetterChannel: It allows message redelivery before sending it to a dead letter endpoint.

- NoErrorHandler: Use it when you do want to use any of the provided error handlers.

For transacted routes we have the TransactionErrorHandler, which is the default error handler for this type of route.

Even though I haven't mentioned error handlers before, we have been working with them. If you take as an example the transacted routes you were testing, if you looked at the logs during the tests, you would have observed log entries like this:

```
[org.apa.cam.jta.TransactionErrorHandler] (vert.x-worker-
thread-3) Transaction rollback (0x2627d493) redelivered(false)
for (MessageId: 0C577FF9615449E-0000000000000001 on ExchangeId:
0C577FF9615449E-0000000000000001) due exchange was marked for
rollbackOnly
```

This is an example of how the `TransactionErrorHandler` works. You didn't have to configure it. Since your route is transacted, if a `TransactionErrorHandler` is not specified, a new one will be created and assigned to that route.

Without further delay, let's see how to configure error handlers.

Start by opening the `camel-dead-letter` project in your IDE. This project has three different `RouteBuilders` and each of them have a different purpose. Let's start with the `RouteBuilder` responsible for declaring the interface you will be interacting with. Open the `RestRoute.java` file shown in Listing 4-21.

Listing 4-21. RestRoute.java File

```java
public class RestRoute extends RouteBuilder {

    @Override
    public void configure() throws Exception {

        rest("/deadLetter")
        .consumes(TEXT_PLAIN)
        .produces(TEXT_PLAIN)
        .post()
        .route()
         .routeId("rest-route")
         .log("Redirecting message")
         .wireTap("seda:process-route")
         .setBody(constant("Thanks!"))
        .endRest();

    }
}
```

In this example, you are exposing a REST interface that accepts a POST request with a text/plain body. The received message is then *wiretapped* to another route using the SEDA component and after that the body is changed before returning a response to the client.

First, let's clarify what wiretap() is. Wire Tap is an integration pattern that allows an exchange to be copied or a new one to be generated using data from the original exchange, and sends it asynchronously to another endpoint. The message pattern here is inOnly because the main route won't be waiting for an endpoint response.

Another thing that is new and highly valuable for route development is SEDA. This component, based on a staged event-driven architecture, will create an in-memory queue so you can process messages in different threads. This way you are asynchronously sending a message copy to be processed by another thread.

Take a look at the RouteBuilder that declares the SEDA consumer shown in Listing 4-22.

Listing 4-22. ProcessRoute.java

```
public class ProcessRoute extends RouteBuilder {

@Override
public void configure() throws Exception {

    errorHandler(deadLetterChannel("seda:dead-letter")
    .maximumRedeliveries(1)
    .useOriginalMessage()
    .onExceptionOccurred(new Processor() {
      @Override
      public void process(Exchange exchange) throws Exception
      {
        log.error("Exception Message : " +
            exchange.getException().getMessage()) ;
```

```
        log.error("Current body:\"" +
            exchange.getMessage().getBody() +"\"");
    }
}));

from("seda:process-route")
.routeId("process-route")
.bean("exceptionBean")
.log("Message Processed with body : ${body}");

    }
}
```

The idea behind this route is to show you different possibilities using error handlers. Here you are declaring a deadLetterChannel error handler and setting a few policies to define how this error handler should work.

There are two ways to declare an error handler, using the route builder scope or using the route scope. In this example, you are using the route builder scope, so if you add another router in this route builder, this new route will also use the defined configuration (unless it is a transacted route). Since this error handler example affects a single route, you could declare it like Listing 4-23.

Listing 4-23. ProcessRoute with Route Scope

```
@Override
public void configure() throws Exception {

from("seda:process-route")
.routeId("process-route")
.errorHandler(deadLetterChannel("seda:dead-letter")
  .maximumRedeliveries(1)
  .useOriginalMessage()
  .onExceptionOccurred(new Processor() {
```

```
    @Override
    public void process(Exchange exchange) throws Exception {
      log.error("Exception Message : " +
        exchange.getException().getMessage());
      log.error("Current body: \"" +
        exchange.getMessage().getBody()+"\"");
    }
  }))
.bean("exceptionBean")
.log("Message Processed with body : ${body}");

  }
}
```

Observe the error handler configuration. The first parameter is to set where the message should be sent after all attempts are made. Here you are going to send the original message, the message sent to the SEDA queue, after one retry to "seda:dead-letter" and as the exception occurs during the retries, a processor will be called to log some information about the exchange.

Let's see what the dead letter route looks like. Open the DeadLetterRoute.java file shown in Listing 4-24.

Listing 4-24. DeadLetterRoute.java File

```
public class DeadLetterRoute extends RouteBuilder {

    @Override
    public void configure() throws Exception {

        from("seda:dead-letter")
        .routeId("dlq-route")
        .log("Problem with request \"${body}\"");

    }

}
```

The only thing that this route does is log the body it receives. This will help me demonstrate how the different configurations are affecting the routing logic.

The last thing left to comment about the process route is the bean being called. This bean will generate exceptions based on the number of processing attempts. Let's examine it. Open the ExceptionBean.java file shown in Listing 4-25.

Listing 4-25. ExceptionBean.java File

```java
@Singleton
@Named("exceptionBean")
@Unremovable
public class ExceptionBean {

    private static final Logger LOG = Logger.getLogger
    (ExceptionBean.class);

    int counter;

    public void analyze(Message message) throws Exception{

        ++counter;

        LOG.info("Attempt Number " + counter);

        message.setBody(UUID.randomUUID().toString());

        if(counter < 3){
            throw new Exception("Not Now!");
        }
    }
}
```

This singleton has an int counter to register the amount of attempts the route has made. It changes the body by setting a random UUID and if the number of attempts is lower than three, it will throw an exception, which will activate the error handler.

So let's give it a try. Open a terminal and run the following command to start the application:

```
camel-dead-letter $ mvn quarkus:dev
```

Once the application is up and running, you can send a request to the REST API like this:

```
$ curl -X POST  http://localhost:8080/deadLetter -H 'Content-
Type: text/plain' -d "testing dead letter"
```

Look at the application log. It will be like Listing 4-26.

Listing 4-26. Application Logs Snippet

```
[rest-route] [INFO] Redirecting message
[co.ap.in.ExceptionBean] [INFO] Attempt Number 1
[co.ap.in.ro.ProcessRoute] [ERROR] Exception Message : Not Now!
[co.ap.in.ro.ProcessRoute] [ERROR] Current body: "7b3cc16c-
d409-4166-b12d-b23299729999"
[co.ap.in.ExceptionBean] [INFO] Attempt Number 2
[co.ap.in.ro.ProcessRoute] [ERROR] Exception Message : Not Now!
[co.ap.in.ro.ProcessRoute] [ERROR] Current body: "2520a0db-
a75c-4324-9f0c-722aa073c60d"
[dlq-route] [INFO] Problem with request "testing dead letter"
```

As you can see in the logs, there were two attempts to make the bean call work. In every attempt, the body was modified before the exception was thrown, but when the error handler reached the limit of retries, the "dlq-route" received the original message and printed it.

You can make a second request, and now no exception will be thrown. You will see a log entry like this:

```
[process-route] [INFO] Message Processed with body : cb65c846-
993a-4835-9e90-f077961f90b2
```

This means that process-route was able to go until its last step.

There are other policies and parameters you can explore, like adding a delay between each retry, using the modified message and sending it to the dead letter address, or even defining until when it should retry based on expression languages. There are many possibilities when setting error handlers. Have this in mind when thinking about how you are going to handle exceptions:

- I put an asynchronous inOnly example on purpose. What I did with the dead letter configuration is not suitable for consumers who need to provide synchronous answers to a client. In the example, we are handling messages that could be processed later, and having a dead letter channel that can persist messages could help to replay them in the future or just with troubleshooting.

- In the example, I forced an exception using a bean, but it could be any component that could throw an exception. In this case, you could use redelivery to reattempt a call to the component. This is particularly interesting when we are accessing an external endpoint that could be momentarily unresponsive.

Let's move on and learn a new way to treat exceptions.

OnException Clause

You saw how to surround a route block using try/catch/finally to treat exceptions. In the error handler examples, it was demonstrated how to treat exceptions in a more generic way, defining error handlers at the route builder level or at the route level. With this new approach, you can still have this broader way to assign handlers and also specialize them based on the exception type. Let's learn about the onException() clause.

In your IDE, open the camel-on-exception project. This project has three route builders that demonstrate different ways to use onException(). Let's start with a non-transacted type of route, so open the OnExceptionRoute.java file shown in Listing 4-27.

Listing 4-27. OnExceptionRoute.java File

```java
public class OnExceptionRoute extends RouteBuilder {

@Override
public void configure() throws Exception {

onException(Exception.class)
.handled(true)
.log(LoggingLevel.ERROR, "Exception Handled")
.setHeader(Exchange.HTTP_RESPONSE_CODE, constant(500))
.setBody(exceptionMessage());

onException(DontLikeException.class)
.handled(true)
.log(LoggingLevel.ERROR,"DontLikeException Handled")
.setHeader(Exchange.HTTP_RESPONSE_CODE, constant(500))
.setBody(constant("There is a problem with apples, try another
fruit."));
```

```
rest("/onException")
  .bindingMode(RestBindingMode.json)
  .post()
    .type(Fruit.class)
    .outType(String.class)
    .consumes(APP_JSON)
    .produces(TEXT_PLAIN)
    .route()
      .routeId("taste-fruit-route")
      .choice()
      .when(simple("${body.name} == 'apple' "))
        .throwException(new DontLikeException())
      .otherwise()
        .throwException(new Exception("Another Problem."))
      .end()
      .log("never get executed.")
    .endRest();
}}
```

You are back with the fruits example, but this time no matter which fruit you choose, an exception will be thrown (but it will have a different response message if you send "apple" in the request.).

The idea here is to show you that you can treat different kinds of exceptions in the same route, and also show you that you can have different scopes for onException() declaration.

Here I am using the route builder scope because there's only a single route and it makes the route readability much better.

The two declared exceptions are handle(), which means that these exceptions won't be propagated back to the caller, in this case the HTTP client. By saying that the exception was handled, if the route is inOut, the

159

execution stops where the exception is thrown and the onException()
block is executed prior to sending a response back to the client. That is why
the line log("never get executed.") will never be executed.

Try this code. From a terminal, start the application:

```
camel-on-exception $ mvn quarkus:dev
```

Once the application gets started, send a request like this:

```
$ curl -w '\n' -X POST http://localhost:8080/onException \
-H 'Content-Type: application/json' -d '{"name": "apple"}'
```

You will get a response like Figure 4-8.

```
~ $ curl -w '\n' -X POST http://localhost:8080/onException \
> -H 'Content-Type: application/json' -d '{"name": "apple"}'
There is a problem with apples, try another fruit.
```

Figure 4-8. *OnException route response*

When it comes to transacted routes, using onException() is not that
different. You just have to remember that you need to mark the route for
rollback. Look at the OnExceptionTransactedRoute.java file example in
Listing 4-28.

Listing 4-28. OnExceptionTransactedRoute.java File

```java
public class OnExceptionTransactedRoute extends RouteBuilder {

@Override
public void configure() throws Exception {
rest("/onExceptionTransacted")
  .bindingMode(RestBindingMode.json)
  .post()
    .type(Fruit.class)
    .outType(String.class)
```

```
    .consumes(APP_JSON)
    .produces(TEXT_PLAIN)
  .route()
    .routeId("save-fruit-route")
    .onException(Exception.class)
     .handled(true)
     .setHeader(Exchange.HTTP_RESPONSE_CODE, constant(500))
     .setHeader(Exchange.CONTENT_TYPE, constant(TEXT_PLAIN))
     .setBody(exceptionMessage())
     .markRollbackOnly()
    .end()
    .transacted()
    .to("jpa:" + Fruit.class.getName())
  .choice()
  .when(simple("${body.name} == 'apple' "))
  .throwException(new Exception("I don't like this fruit"))
  .otherwise()
     .setHeader(Exchange.CONTENT_TYPE,constant(TEXT_PLAIN))
     .setBody(constant("I like this fruit!"))
  .endRest()
 .get()
 .outType(List.class)
 .produces(APP_JSON)
 .route()
  .routeId("list-fruits")
  .to("jpa:"+Fruit.class.getName()+"?query={{query.all}}" );

 }
}
```

In this example, you are using onException() in a route scope and,
as in the previous example, marking the exception as handled(true). In
the onException() block, you prepare a response to the client by setting

headers and the message body. Once you finish setting what you need, you set the exchange to rollback.

This route works just like the try/catch example. It will roll back any entry with "apple" and any entry that has a name previously persisted. It also has a GET operation so you can check the values in the database.

With the application still running, send a request that will be accepted by the API:

```
$ curl -X POST http://localhost:8080/onExceptionTransacted \
-H 'Content-Type: application/json' -d '{"name": "grape"}'
```

Repeat the same request, and after that try to send a request with "apple":

```
$ curl -X POST http://localhost:8080/onExceptionTransacted \
-H 'Content-Type: application/json' -d '{"name": "apple"}'
```

Now you can check how many fruits there are in the database:

```
$ curl http://localhost:8080/onExceptionTransacted
```

Only the first non-apple request will be persisted, so you will receive a list with a single item in it, like this:

```
[{"id":1,"name":"grape"}]
```

There is one example left to explore on how to handle exceptions with Camel. This time you are going to handle the exception and continue the original routing as the exception didn't occur.

Open the OnExceptionContinuedRoute.java file from Listing 4-29 in your IDE.

Listing 4-29. OnExceptionContinuedRoute.java

```java
public class OnExceptionContinuedRoute extends RouteBuilder {

@Override
public void configure() throws Exception {

onException(Exception.class)
.continued(true)
.log(LoggingLevel.ERROR, "Exception Handled")
.setHeader(Exchange.HTTP_RESPONSE_CODE, constant(500))
.setBody(exceptionMessage());

rest("/onExceptionContinued")
  .bindingMode(RestBindingMode.json)
  .post()
  .type(Fruit.class)
  .outType(String.class)
  .consumes(APP_JSON)
  .produces(TEXT_PLAIN)
  .route()
    .routeId("continued-route")
    .choice()
    .when(simple("${body.name} == 'apple' "))
.throwException(new DontLikeException("Try another Fruit."))
    .otherwise()
      .setBody(constant("I like this fruit."))
    .end()
    .setHeader(Exchange.CONTENT_TYPE, constant(TEXT_PLAIN))
    .log("Gets Executed.")
  .endRest();

    }
}
```

This code is a simplified version of OnExceptionRoute, as I only need one onException() clause to show how continued() works. As you can see, instead of using handled() you are using continued(), which means that the exception will be caught, the onException() block will get executed, and then you will go back to the original routing on the point the exception was thrown. This is why you're setting the content type header after the choice. It doesn't matter if you get an exception or not; this last piece of code will get executed.

With the application running, try to send an "apple" in the request:

```
curl -X POST http://localhost:8080/onExceptionContinued \
-H 'Content-Type: application/json' -d '{"name": "apple"}'
```

You will receive a treated response as in the previous examples, but look at the application logs. You will find the log entry that was the last part of the route, showing you that the original routing continued. The log entry will look like this:

```
2021-05-31 08:56:55,224 INFO  [continued-route] (vert.x-worker-
thread-1) Gets Executed.
```

You explored the three different ways to perform error handling in Camel. Of course there are more configurations that can be applied in each of these mechanisms, but here you explored the main aspects and cases of error handling. Once each of them are understood, you will be able to choose the best one for your given use case.

Summary

In this chapter, you focused on how to persist and consume data from relational databases and the techniques to maintain that data consistently when manipulating it. As you progressed you saw the different ways to perform error handling using Camel.

You learned the following topics in this chapter:

- How to configure data sources and hibernate using Quarkus

- How to use the `camel-quarkus-jpa` to persist and consume data from relational databases

- How to configure JTA transactions using Quarkus and Camel

- Different strategies for error handling for both transacted and non-transacted routes

In the next chapter, we will focus on asynchronous communication using messaging and the architectural possibilities that this approach brings with it.

CHAPTER 5

Messaging with Apache Kafka

In the previous chapters, we focused essentially on the use of synchronous methods for cross-application communication, more specifically REST. Although REST (and its ecosystem) is very rich in features and can support many different use cases, it is not as scalable and resilient as some asynchronous communication patterns. Synchronous communication requires the backend to be available to respond immediately to the clients' calls, but some services may take more time to respond due to their complexity or may even depend on other services, which can generate a timeout chain where one service in a chain can become a bottleneck and make requests start to fail.

As in the stateful vs. stateless discussion, where we ideally try to be stateless because of the many benefits of a stateless architecture, we know that not every application can be stateless. The same is true for some processes and services that must be executed synchronously. The idea is to understand how asynchronous communication works, which patterns we have at our disposal, and how we can implement them. We can take reactive programming or event-driven programming as an example of how asynchronous processing can be beneficial to application performance. It means that no component needs to be waiting for another component to finish its task, so instead of waiting it could be executing something else.

© Guilherme Camposo 2021
G. Camposo, *Cloud Native Integration with Apache Camel*,
https://doi.org/10.1007/978-1-4842-7211-4_5

In this chapter, we will dive into asynchronous communication using a messaging system. The tool of choice is another Apache Foundation project, the Apache Kafka. You will learn when and how you should use asynchronous communication using messaging while you learn how to implement it using Kafka and Camel.

Message-Oriented Middleware

Message-oriented middleware (MOMs) are systems specialized in receiving and dispatching data in the format of messages. They serve as a man in the middle that guarantees that a message was received from a producer and that the message will be available and properly delivered to a consumer. Let's discuss how this kind of system works and what we can get from it.

Before talking about MOMs, we first need to define messaging. It may sound redundant to talk about messaging because this concept is something very present in our lives. Email, texting apps, and even the postal service can serve as a good analogy of what messaging means, which is *using a service to deliver a message between entities*. Another characteristic of messaging is that the producer, or the message sender, does not need to wait for the consumer, or the message receiver, to acknowledge that it received the message. The mediation of message production and message consumption is done by the middleware layer. It is the middleware layer that acknowledges message delivery to the producer and once it has it, the layer will have mechanisms to guarantee that the message will reach its destination. This frees the producer to perform other tasks without having to wait for the consumer, while the consumer can consume messages at its own pace.

Besides the characteristics of asynchronous communication, the use of MOMs allows other possibilities because of its patterns. One that we can highlight is how the use of MOMs can improve service composability.

Composability is a design principle that analyzes how services can connect to each other to create combinations that can serve new use cases. To clarify what this means, let's put this concept into a real life example. Think about social media. It all started as a way for people to connect. You wanted to know how your family was, what your friends were doing, or even to get to know new people. Now compare that with what it has become. It's now a platform for public figures, from politicians to pop artists, where you can buy or sell anything, watch events such as live music shows or sports, and so on. It grew so much in services and capacities that we feel that all aspects of our lives are handled there. And this was possible because of the way people's data is handled. Of course this is a very overwhelming example because it brings much more than just the notion of composability but it serves the purpose of exemplifying what it means.

MOMs usually work with the concept of destination, which is the address where messages are sent. This destination is not something present in the producer or in the consumer, but a register in the messaging system or message broker, making it a way to improve composability by promoting decoupling. The producer doesn't know who is consuming messages from a destination, and the consumer doesn't know who is sending messages. This way we can add more producers to that destination if they can produce the expected data or we can add more consumers if the data is relevant for more applications. Observe that this communication is more about the data being exchanged than the component's relationship. A good domain design is imperative to achieve better levels of composability.

Destinations are usually categorized into two types: queues and topics. Let's discuss them individually.

Queues are destinations made for communication channels where the receiver is generally a single application. They are like email inboxes. They can receive messages from anyone, but only the email owner will be able to access that information. Messages stay in the queue until they get consumed by the appropriate receiver or until rules like "time to live,"

169

where messages are purged based on how long they are in the queue, get active. You can see a representation of a queue in Figure 5-1.

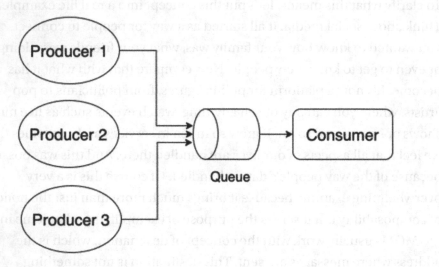

Figure 5-1. *Queue representation*

On the other hand, topics are communication channels made for broadcasting messages. Different consumers can subscribe to a topic and once any message is available, all of them (if no filtering is configured) will receive a copy of that message. You can see a topic representation in Figure 5-2.

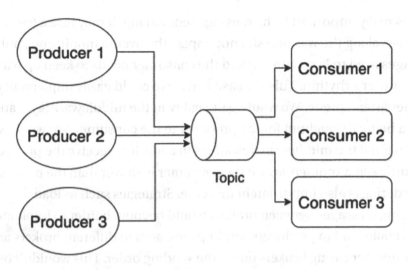

Figure 5-2. *Topic representation*

This is an overall representation of the main concepts in messaging. Depending on the product or language you are using, you might have different names for these concepts. Here I'm using the Jakarta Messaging (formerly JMS, Java Messaging) specification nomenclature. The specification itself abstracts these concepts, independently of vendor or implementation, in a common API to be used by the Java language, so it's fair to use this nomenclature when we use Java to create integrations with messaging.

Talking about implementation, there are other aspects of queues and topics that we have to take into consideration, and persistence may be the main one.

Queues and topics can be persistent or not. It will all depend on the producers' and consumers' relationships and the nature of the data. Take as an example a device responsible for monitoring a truck location. It will send a notification message from time to time to inform the truck's current coordinates. Depending on how the truck is moving, if it is stopped in traffic or if it is refueling, you might receive a lot of messages with the same coordinates. For this scenario, not every message is critical.

What is really important is the message sequencing. It may lose a few messages along the way and still not impact the overall monitoring, but messages need to keep coming and the consumer needs to keep up with the producer's rhythm. This is a case where we could easily implement a non-persistent queue. We would gain agility in the middleware layer and allow a better throughput for the producer to the consumer. We would still need to mind the middleware resources to allow it to receive the producers' load and keep it momentarily if the consumer is slower than the producer.

Ordering is also important in this case. Strategies such as load balancing messages between brokers would become harder to implement, as this could lead to producers sending messages to different brokers and consumers accessing brokers out of the sending order. This wouldn't be a problem if we had a different case, though.

Imagine that we have an e-commerce website that places customer orders in a queue for processing. Ordering is not a problem in this case because each order is a completely isolated event. So we could easily distribute this load by load balancing, but each event is important and cannot be missed. For this case, we need a persistent queue to guarantee that we have mechanisms to recover messages in case of broker failure since we cannot risk losing messages.

Topics also have similar requirements. The more traditional implementation makes the topic a broadcast mechanism for subscribers that are available at the moment the message is received by the broker, so the message is not really persisted, but still there are situations where we need to broadcast messages and guarantee that consumers can get them later. Traditional messaging is about consuming messages. Once the message is processed, it gets erased from the destination. It would be harder for topics to completely adopt this mechanism since it would be difficult to expect that all subscribers read a particular entry or to add more subscribers at any given time and still be consistent. To solve problems where persistence is required for topics, different products implement different mechanisms, from routing messages from topics to persistent queues created specifically for the subscriber, to not erasing messages based on reads but time or storage space, as you are going to see later.

High availability, performance, data replication, scalability, monitoring, and other factors will guide you to a specific implementation of a message broker. We won't be discussing these characteristics in isolation; we will talk about them when describing Apache Kafka.

Apache Kafka

So let's bring the message broker theory to reality by materializing it in an implementation product. You'll learn Kafka core concepts and characteristics before learning how to use them with Camel.

In the words of the project web page, "Apache Kafka is an open-source distributed event streaming platform". Let's break down some of those words to understand what they really mean. Starting with "event streaming", an event, in a broader sense, is data generated by one source that is captured or received by a consumer that will process that data at some level. Some examples of event sources are sensors, database changes, webhooks, applications calls, and so on. They all generate data that can trigger other applications. Streaming means that those events occur continuously and possibility with high volumetry.

To understand the distributed part, you need to understand Kafka's architecture first.

Concepts and Architecture

There is a lot of hype around Kafka. Big tech companies are using it, saying that they are dealing with billions of transactions a day, moving around terabytes of data, which will obviously catch the attention of the developers and architects who need to build a resilient and high performance solution for their intra services communication. So let's learn what Kafka is really about and then you can draw your own conclusions.

Kafka was created by LinkedIn before becoming open source in 2011. It was originally designed to deal with big streams of data, like tracking page view events to gathering aggregated logs from services. You may ask yourself, why would LinkedIn create a messaging system with so many available in the market? Well, it needed a robust and scalable platform to deal with a very high volumetry with very low latency, so some major design decisions had to be made to achieve that.

Kafka only offers persistent topics. As I stated before, you may need a different strategy to allow persistent topics, since it is hard to synchronize how consumers read messages in the topic, so erasing them based on reading becomes complicated. In Kafka, messages are not consumed, they are rotated based on storage utilization or based on how long the message is persisted.

This single design choice opens up new possibilities. Since everything is a topic, we can add more consumers to a destination as needed and consumers will be able to pick up messages that were there before they started subscribing. Although this may be the desired behavior for some cases, it might not be for other cases where a consumer doesn't want to receive old messages. And what if a current consumer goes offline? How would it resume from where it started? Kafka keeps message indexes using a structure called **offset**, as you can see in Figure 5-3.

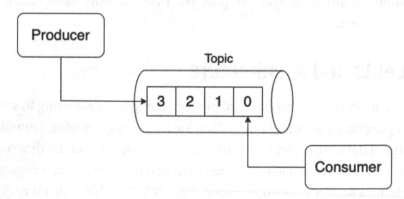

Figure 5-3. *Offset representation*

Offset are sequential long values used by Kafka to mark a message position. They are used to identify which message was read for a **consumer group** (we will get to consumer groups later).

Message disposition in Kafka is somewhat different. Topics are divided into **partitions**. Each partition is an independent structure that stores the topic messages. To materialize this explanation, imagine a Kafka cluster with two brokers (Kafka instances), as in Figure 5-4.

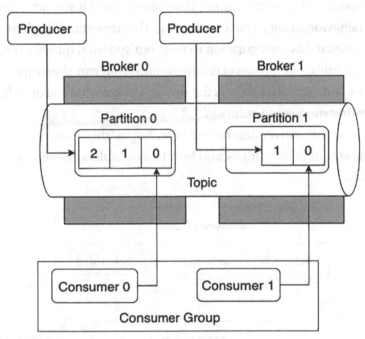

Figure 5-4. *Kafka partition distribution*

In this example, there is a single topic with two partitions spread between two brokers. Each partition is independent, receiving isolated writes from producers and providing reads for consumers. Each partition has its own offset counting and that offset is used for consumer groups to identify which message was read in that partition. Consumer group allows different instances of the same consumer application to parallelize readings without having duplication. In this example, each consumer in the consumer group is assigned to a partition and only that consumer will

175

read from that partition. If this consumer gets dropped out and a new one, for the same consumer group, is assigned, the new one can start reading from where the old consumer stopped.

As you can see, topics in Kafka are essentially a group of partitions. Partitions are a great design choice to allow parallel and distributed processing. We set the number of partitions we need in the topic creation, but we can also add more partitions later. The number of partitions is a decision based on expected volumetry, expected response time, cluster arrangement, consumer behavior, storage space, and so on. The important idea here is the flexibility to adjust this configuration to meet our system requirements.

There is a bunch of low-level configurations that can also impact performance but our focus here is the design choices that make Kafka a very interesting messaging solution.

Continuing our conversion on the meaning of "distributed" in Kafka's description, you need to understand how to assemble a cluster. Take a look at Figure 5-5.

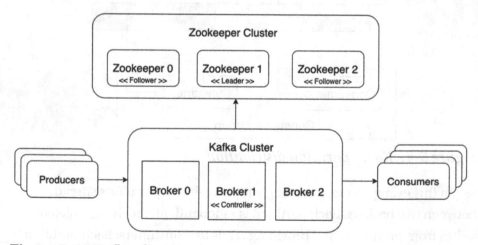

Figure 5-5. *Kafka cluster*

One of the first things a Kafka instance does when starting up is to register itself in a Zookeeper instance. Zookeeper is a coordination service for distributed applications, which means that it provides common services like naming, configuration management, synchronization, and group services. Kafka utilizes Zookeeper to manage information about cluster members, topics, access control lists, and a very important task, the election of the Kafka **controller**, the Kafka instance that will be the brain behind the cluster automation.

> *The version 2.8.0 provides an early access version of KIP-500, which allows you to run Kafka brokers without Apache ZooKeeper, but this is not production ready, that is why I'm talking about Zookeeper here.*

Zookeeper is an important piece in this architecture because it enables high availability to a cluster by providing coordination. Zookeeper is also HA. It utilizes an election process, and once a leader is elected, incoming write requests are always processed by the leader, who requests the same write to all available nodes. If a quorum is met, that request is considered successful.

When we talk about a high availability in systems we are not just talking about service availability, but also about data availability, especially for a system that behaves like a database. Kafka addresses this necessity with a functionality called **replicas**. Look at Figure 5-6 to check how Kafka can replicate partition data.

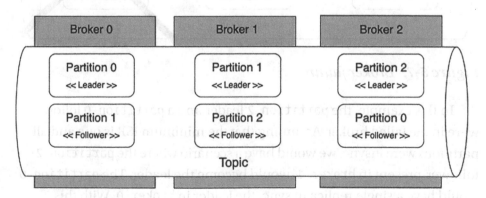

Figure 5-6. Kafka replicas

In the example above, there is a single topic with three partitions distributed between three brokers. What's new is that each partition is replicated, so it is a topic with three partitions and two replicas.

I said earlier that each partition is independent and will receive isolated write requests and that is still true, even when we have more than one replica. What happens is that the controller has to elect one of the partition replicas as the leader. Only the leader receives requests for writing and reading, and it is responsible for sending write requests to the followers to keep the replicas consistent. This process is highly monitored and its status is represented through the **ISR** (In-Sync Replicas) value. You will see this value display in a few pages. Ideally, partition replicas won't be in the same broker, this way we have data redundancy in case a broker fail.

Continuing with the example above, imagine that one broker goes down. We would have a situation like Figure 5-7.

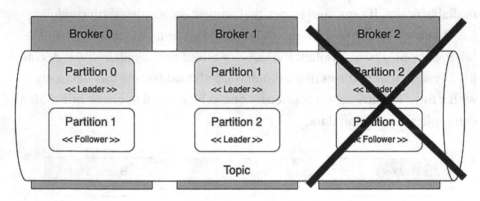

Figure 5-7. *Broker failure*

In this example, the partition 2 leader and a partition 0 follower were in the failed broker. Assuming that the minimum ISR is one and all partitions were insync, we would have a scenario where the partition 2 follower, present in broker 1, would become the leader. The partition 0 would have a single replica in sync, the leader in broker 0. With this configuration, no data would be lost and the service would still be available for all partitions.

178

There are more concepts and possible configurations to discuss, but the idea here is to set a basic understanding of Kafka's architecture and why it is interesting before you start using it. These are the major concepts that everyone working with Kafka needs to understand.

Next, you will see how to install and use one instance locally.

Installing and Running

You learned about Kafka's basic concepts and now it's time to try the tool. It can be configured to create huge clusters to support a multitude of producers and consumers exchanging a great amount of data, but, as usual, we will start small, with an example that you can easily run in your dev setup.

You used Docker to facilitate your experience with Keycloak and you will do the same with Kafka. Unfortunately the project doesn't offer a ready-to-use container image, but we can count on the community to provide one for us. You will use the `wurstmeister/kafka` image. Under the `kafka-installation` folder is the git project of the images used in this example, `kafka-docker` and `zookeeper-docker`, in case you want to know how these images were built or even to build them yourself. In the same folder you will find a `docker-compose.yml` file that you will use to start the application. Open this file in your IDE or text editor. Let's take a look at it; see Listing 5-1.

Listing 5-1. Kafka docker-compose.yml

```
version: '3'
services:
  zookeeper:
    image: wurstmeister/zookeeper:latest
    container_name: zookeeper
    environment:
```

179

```
        ZOOKEEPER_CLIENT_PORT: 2181
        ZOOKEEPER_TICK_TIME: 2000
    ports:
        - 22181:2181

  kafka:
    image: wurstmeister/kafka:2.13-2.7.0
    container_name: broker
    depends_on:
      - zookeeper
    ports:
    - 9092:9092
    environment:
      KAFKA_ADVERTISED_HOST_NAME: localhost
      KAFKA_ZOOKEEPER_CONNECT: zookeeper:2181
```

For this example, you are using Docker compose because Kafka needs a Zookeeper instance to connect to, so you define two services in the document, zookeeper and kafka. For a basic experience of how Kafka works and to use it to exchange messages between applications, you won't need a cluster, which is why you are setting this compose file to only allow a single instance by fixing a container name in each service. It will also help you with the docker commands you will need to perform.

Let's start Kafka. In a terminal, navigate to the kafka-installation folder and run the following command:

```
kafka-installation $ docker compose up -d
```

Once it finishes downloading the images, you should get a visualization like Figure 5-8.

```
gcamposo:kafka-installation $ docker compose up -d
[+] Running 2/2
 ⠿ Container zookeeper  Started                                          3.1s
 ⠿ Container broker     Started                                          6.7s
```

Figure 5-8. *docker compose up result*

To check if Kafka is properly started, look at the container logs with the following command:

```
$ docker logs broker
```

Look for log entries like Listing 5-2. If you find them, this means that Kafka is ready to go.

Listing 5-2. Kafka Container Log Snippet

```
...
[2021-06-05 15:30:28,450] INFO [KafkaServer id=1001] started
(kafka.server.KafkaServer)
[2021-06-05 15:30:28,506] INFO [broker-1001-to-controller-send-
thread]: Recorded new controller, from now on will use broker
1001 (kafka.server.BrokerToControllerRequestThread)
```

Kafka doesn't come with a visualization tool or console, although there are many projects and vendors that provide this kind of functionality, but it comes with a collection of scripts that will allow you to manage it.

Start by accessing the broker container to visualize the script collection. Run the following command from a terminal:

```
$ docker exec -it broker /bin/sh
```

From this point on you can navigate to where Kafka was installed in this image. Here the installation path is /opt/kafka. Go to this folder with the command:

```
/ # cd /opt/kafka/bin/
```

Once in the directory, list it. You will get a result like Figure 5-9.

```
/opt/kafka_2.13-2.7.0/bin # ls
connect-distributed.sh              kafka-preferred-replica-election.sh
connect-mirror-maker.sh             kafka-producer-perf-test.sh
connect-standalone.sh               kafka-reassign-partitions.sh
kafka-acls.sh                       kafka-replica-verification.sh
kafka-broker-api-versions.sh        kafka-run-class.sh
kafka-configs.sh                    kafka-server-start.sh
kafka-console-consumer.sh           kafka-server-stop.sh
kafka-console-producer.sh           kafka-streams-application-reset.sh
kafka-consumer-groups.sh            kafka-topics.sh
kafka-consumer-perf-test.sh         kafka-verifiable-consumer.sh
kafka-delegation-tokens.sh          kafka-verifiable-producer.sh
kafka-delete-records.sh             trogdor.sh
kafka-dump-log.sh                   windows
kafka-features.sh                   zookeeper-security-migration.sh
kafka-leader-election.sh            zookeeper-server-start.sh
kafka-log-dirs.sh                   zookeeper-server-stop.sh
kafka-mirror-maker.sh               zookeeper-shell.sh
```

Figure 5-9. *Kafka's scripts*

There is a lot of different configurations that can be made using these scripts, but you will only perform some basic operations that will help you to utilize Kafka for messaging.

The first step is to create a topic. Run the following command to create a topic:

```
/opt/kafka_2.13-2.7.0/bin # kafka-topics.sh \
--bootstrap-server localhost:9092 --create \
--replication-factor 1 --partitions 2 --topic myTestTopic
```

Expect the "Created topic myTestTopic." message as the result.

You can use the kafka-topics.sh to find more operations related to topic management, for example, listing the existent topic in the cluster:

```
/opt/kafka_2.13-2.7.0/bin # kafka-topics.sh \
--bootstrap-server localhost:9092 --list
```

This operation only shows the topic names so you know they exist, but if you need more information regarding a topic, you can describe it, like in the following command:

```
/opt/kafka_2.13-2.7.0/bin # kafka-topics.sh \
--bootstrap-server localhost:9092 --describe \
--topic myTestTopic
```

If you run this command, you get a result like Figure 5-10.

```
/opt/kafka_2.13-2.7.0/bin # kafka-topics.sh \
> --bootstrap-server localhost:9092 --describe \
> --topic myTestTopic
Topic: myTestTopic      PartitionCount: 2       ReplicationFactor: 1    Configs: segment.bytes=10
73741824
        Topic: myTestTopic      Partition: 0    Leader: 1001    Replicas: 1001  Isr: 1001
        Topic: myTestTopic      Partition: 1    Leader: 1001    Replicas: 1001  Isr: 1001
```

Figure 5-10. *Topic describe command*

This command shows many important things about the topic, like its number of partitions, replication factor, and specific configurations it may have, but it is the second line that is really interesting. It shows where the partitions are, who is the leader, where the replicas are, and which replicas are insync. In the example, there are two partitions but a single broker instance. In this case, the partition leaders are in the broker with id 1001 (you saw that in the startup log), so there is a single replica per partition, which is the partition leader itself.

You can also alter this entity configuration. Let's say you want to set the retention period of a topic to 10 seconds. You could do it like this:

```
/opt/kafka_2.13-2.7.0/bin # kafka-configs.sh \
--bootstrap-server localhost:9092 \
--topic myTestTopic --alter --add-config retention.ms=10000
```

Then you could check the topic again and see if the command above had some effect. Run the describe command again, like in Figure 5-11.

```
/opt/kafka_2.13-2.7.0/bin # kafka-topics.sh --bootstrap-server localhost:9092 --describe --topic
myTestTopic
Topic: myTestTopic        PartitionCount: 2        ReplicationFactor: 1    Configs: segment.bytes=10
73741824,retention.ms=10000
        Topic: myTestTopic       Partition: 0    Leader: 1001    Replicas: 1001  Isr: 1001
        Topic: myTestTopic       Partition: 1    Leader: 1001    Replicas: 1001  Isr: 1001
```

Figure 5-11. *Altered topic*

The change was applied. You can see that there is a new configuration for that topic retention period.

Testing the Installation

Now that you have a running Kafka broker, you need to start testing it using applications. You will use Camel to access Kafka in just a bit, but first let's leverage some applications provided by the Kafka installation.

I hope you still have that terminal open with the broker container. If not, just follow the steps of the previous section, because you are going to use two scripts in there: `kafka-console-producer.sh` and `kafka-console-consumer.sh`.

Let's start by setting the consumer app. In the terminal you already have open, in the `kafka/bin` directory, run the following command:

```
/opt/kafka_2.13-2.7.0/bin # kafka-console-consumer.sh \
--bootstrap-server localhost:9092 --topic myTestTopic
```

At this moment the command line is frozen, waiting for messages to start to come on the topic, so let's prepare the producer. Open a new terminal, access the broker container, and go to the `/opt/kafka/bin` directory. Run the producer script like this:

```
/opt/kafka_2.13-2.7.0/bin # kafka-console-producer.sh
--bootstrap-server localhost:9092 --topic myTestTopic
```

A cursor will be open for you. Type a message and press Enter. Then check your consumer. It will receive the exact message you sent.

Stop the consumer and producer by pressing Control + C. You will perform a new test now. First, let's increase the retention period, setting it back to the default value, which is seven days. Run the following command:

```
/opt/kafka_2.13-2.7.0/bin # kafka-configs.sh \
--bootstrap-server localhost:9092 --topic myTestTopic \
--alter --config retention.ms=60480000
```

Open the producer again. Send three messages like this:

- helloworld

- producer

- consumer

Now open the consumer like you did before. You won't get any message. This happens because this consumer is configured to only read new messages. Add the option -from-beginning and you will get those messages, like in Figure 5-12.

```
/opt/kafka_2.13-2.7.0/bin # kafka-console-consumer.sh --bootstrap-server
localhost:9092 --from-beginning --topic myTestTopic
helloworld
consumer
producer
```

Figure 5-12. *Reading old offsets*

This section shows what looks like to connect applications using Kafka as the message broker. Those scripts can help you to debug because they can receive different configurations, like consuming a particular partition or using a given group id.

Camel and Kafka

You just learned about Kafka's concepts and architecture, how to perform basic operations, and how to run a basic test. Now you will connect a Camel application and discuss some caveats of this kind of implementation.

In the first example of using Camel to access Kafka topics, you will use two different applications: `camel-kafka-producer` and `camel-kafka-consumer`. The producer will expose a REST interface to enable you to send messages to the consumer application. With this simple setup you will explore some configurations for producers and consumers with the Kafka component.

Setting Up the Application

Let's see what it takes to configure a Camel application to access a Kafka topic.

Start by analyzing the `camel-kafka-producer` code. Load it in your favorite IDE. Look at the pom file in Listing 5-3.

Listing 5-3. pom.xml Snippet

```
...
<dependencies>
<dependency>
<groupId>org.apache.camel.quarkus</groupId>
<artifactId>camel-quarkus-kafka</artifactId>
</dependency>
<dependency>
<groupId>org.apache.camel.quarkus</groupId>
<artifactId>camel-quarkus-rest</artifactId>
```

```
</dependency>
</dependencies>
...
```

You only have two dependencies for this project, `camel-quarkus-rest` and `camel-quarkus-kafka`. The REST component you already know. It will be responsible for adding the webserver implementation and enabling the REST DSL. The Kafka component is your object of study. Let's see what this project route looks like. Open the `RestKafkaRoute.java` file shown in Listing 5-4.

Listing 5-4. RestKafkaRoute.java File

```java
public class RestKafkaRoute extends RouteBuilder {

@Override
public void configure() throws Exception {

  rest("/kafka")
  .consumes(TEXT_PLAIN)
  .produces(TEXT_PLAIN)
  .post()
  .route()
    .routeId("rest-route")
    .log("sending message.")
    .removeHeaders("*")
    .to("{{kafka.uri}}")
    .removeHeaders("*")
    .setBody(constant("message sent."))
    .log("${body}")
  .endRest();
}}
```

This route receives a `text/plain` body, sends it to a Kafka topic, and gets back a response informing that the message was sent to the topic, but there is something in the middle of this logic that you haven't done before. Right before the Kafka component step, you are removing the message headers using a catch-all pattern. This is something that you didn't do before because the cases you were facing weren't impacted by header propagation.

Depending on the component, it may have some special header that it will react to, for example, the JPA query parameter, but for this component other headers are completely ignored. In this case, you are working with a component that is more sensitive to headers because the application being invoked has headers in its data model.

Kafka messages (a.k.a.records) are key-value pair entries with some metadata plus messages headers. The key is an optional field used for partition assignment. The value is the actual message you want to send.

In the example, you remove all the of headers coming from the HTTP request because you won't need them and you don't want to send useless information to Kafka. After the component call you also remove the headers because again you don't need the returned information and you don't want to expose Kafka information to the HTTP client.

You may have noticed the property key used to declare the endpoint configuration. Since this component needs more configuration than the previous examples, it makes sense to use the `application.properties` file to improve this code readability and configurability.

Open the properties file (Listing 5-5) in your IDE.

Listing 5-5. application.properties File

```
topic=example1
brokers=localhost:9092
id=producer
kafka.uri=kafka:{{topic}}?brokers={{brokers}}&clientId={{id}}
```

The Kafka component requires a few parameters to work properly. The first one is the topic it will send messages to. Here you are setting "example1" as the value. You will create this topic later. You also need to set the brokers addresses. If you were connecting to a cluster, you would have to configure a list in this parameter. The Kafka client needs to know all members of the cluster so it can access them depending on the partition distribution or load balancing. The clientId in this situation will help Kafka and you to trace calls.

Now, let's look at the consumer application. Open the camel-kafka-consumer project in your IDE. Look at the RouteBuilder in Listing 5-6.

Listing 5-6. KafkaConsumerRoute.java File

```java
public class KafkaConsumerRoute extends RouteBuilder {

    @Override
    public void configure() throws Exception {

        from("{{kafka.uri}}")
        .routeId("consumer-route")
        .log("Headers : ${headers}")
        .log("Body : ${body}");
    }
}
```

This route consumes messages from a topic and logs the message content, first its headers and then the message content.

Let's look this project's application.properties in Listing 5-7.

Listing 5-7. camel-kafka-consumer Project's application.properties File

```
topic=example1
brokers=localhost:9092
kafka.uri=kafka:{{topic}}?brokers={{brokers}}&clientId=${kafka.
clientid}&groupId=${kafka.groupid}
```

This configuration is similar to what you saw before. The only difference is that for consumers it is recommended to set a groupId. Group ids allow you to persist the offsets read, so if you restart the consumer application, it will be able to restart from where it stopped. The clientId and groupId use property markers as values because you are going to pass these parameters as JVM variables to the application.

First Test

You saw how the example applications are configured. Now you need to see how they will behave in different scenarios.

Let's test the code. Before running the applications, you need to create the "example1" topic. You can run the following command to do it:

```
docker exec -it broker /opt/kafka/bin/kafka-topics.sh \
--create --bootstrap-server localhost:9092 \
--replication-factor 1 --partitions 2 --topic example1
```

With the topic created, you can start the consumer. In a terminal, under the camel-kafka-consumer directory, run the following command:

```
camel-kafka-consumer/ $ mvn quarkus:dev -Dkafka.
clientid=test   -Dkafka.groupid=testGroup
```

With the consumer started, look at the consumer logs. There is some interesting information there. They will look like this:

```
[Consumer clientId=test, groupId=testGroup] Notifying assignor
about the new Assignment(partitions=[example1-0, example1-1])
```

The log entry identifies the consumer by its `clientId` and `groupId` in the assignment process, which is the process that determines which partition a member of a consumer group will get messages from. In this case, since you only have a single consumer and two partitions, the consumer will get messages from both partitions.

```
[Consumer clientId=test, groupId=testGroup] Found no committed
offset for partition example1-0
[Consumer clientId=test, groupId=testGroup] Found no committed
offset for partition example1-1
```

The messages above tell you that there are no offset readings saved for both partitions.

```
[Consumer clientId=test, groupId=testGroup] Resetting offset
for partition example1-0 to position FetchPosition{offset=0,
offsetEpoch=Optional.empty, currentLeader=LeaderAndEpoch{leader
=Optional[localhost:9092 (id: 1001 rack: null)], epoch=0}}.
```

```
[Consumer clientId=test, groupId=testGroup] Resetting offset
for partition example1-1 to position FetchPosition{offset=0,
offsetEpoch=Optional.empty, currentLeader=LeaderAndEpoch{leader
=Optional[localhost:9092 (id: 1001 rack: null)], epoch=0}}.
```

These entries tell you from which offset you will start reading messages, in this case `offset=0`. They also tell who the leader is for the given partition, in this case `localhost:9092 (id: 1001)`.

You can start the producer now. In a new terminal, run the following command:

```
camel-kafka-producer/ $ mvn quarkus:dev -Ddebug=5006
```

With the producer started you can send a request to it. Send the following request:

```
$ curl  -X POST 'http://localhost:8080/kafka'    \
-H 'Content-Type: text/plain' -d 'Testing Kafka'
```

Look at the consumer logs. You will get something like this:

```
2021-06-06 08:47:42,524 INFO  [consumer-route] (Camel (camel-1)
thread #0 - KafkaConsumer[example1]) Headers : {kafka.
HEADERS=RecordHeaders(headers = [], isReadOnly = false), kafka.
OFFSET=0, kafka.PARTITION=1, kafka.TIMESTAMP=1622980062458,
kafka.TOPIC=example1}

2021-06-06 08:47:42,528 INFO  [consumer-route] (Camel (camel-1)
thread #0 - KafkaConsumer[example1]) Body : Testing Kafka
```

The first log entry is the values of message headers. As you can see, the consumer will return some information regarding the reading, like the offset read, which partition, which topic, and the message timestamp, which will tell you when the message got in the topic. The second value is the actual message.

Let's try again with a different message:

```
$ curl  -X POST 'http://localhost:8080/kafka'\
 -H 'Content-Type: text/plain' -d 'Learning Camel'
```

Look at the consumer logs again. You will see entries like this:

```
2021-06-06 08:49:22,988 INFO  [consumer-route] (Camel (camel-1)
thread #0 - KafkaConsumer[example1]) Headers : {kafka.
HEADERS=RecordHeaders(headers = [], isReadOnly = false), kafka.
OFFSET=0, kafka.PARTITION=0, kafka.TIMESTAMP=1622980162982,
kafka.TOPIC=example1}
```

```
2021-06-06 08:49:22,989 INFO  [consumer-route] (Camel (camel-1)
thread #0 - KafkaConsumer[example1]) Body : Learning Camel
```

The partition is different from the previous test, but still the consumer
is getting messages from both partitions. Let's add a new consumer to the
same consumer group.

Open a new terminal. Navigate to the camel-kafka-consumer project
directory and run the following command:

```
camel-kafka-consumer/ $ mvn quarkus:dev -Dkafka.
clientId=other  -Dkafka.groupid=testGroup -Ddebug=5007
```

Once the application has started, look at its logs. Here is my example:

```
[Consumer clientId=other, groupId=testGroup] Adding newly
assigned partitions: example1-0
```

```
[Consumer clientId=other, groupId=testGroup] Setting
offset for partition example1-0 to the committed offset
FetchPosition{offset=1, offsetEpoch=Optional.empty, currentLe
ader=LeaderAndEpoch{leader=Optional[localhost:9092 (id: 1001
rack: null)], epoch=0}}
```

The partition 0 was assigned for my new consumer and it will start
reading from the offset=1. If you look at the logs on the first consumer,
you will see that now only one partition is assigned to it.

Scaling Consumers

We discussed how scalable Kafka's architecture is, but to scale in this context also means to increase processing capacity on the consumer side. When thinking about how to scale consumers there are some rules we need to follow.

What would happen if we added a new consumer to the same group? Let's try. Open a new terminal in the camel-kafka-consumer directory and run the following command:

```
camel-kafka-consumer/ $ mvn quarkus:dev -Dkafka.
clientid=third  -Dkafka.groupid=testGroup -Ddebug=5008
```

Once the application started, this is what happened to my new consumer:

```
[Consumer clientId=third, groupId=testGroup] Notifying assignor
about the new Assignment(partitions=[])
```

No partition was assigned to it. Let's check what happens when you add messages to the topic. Run the following bash script to enter ten new messages in the topic.

```
$ i=0; while [ $i -lt 10 ]; do ((i++)); curl -w "\n" -X
POST 'http://localhost:8080/kafka' -H 'Content-Type: text/
plain'   -d "Message number: $i" ; done
```

If you look at the consumers' logs, you will see that the consumer without a partition assigned is not receiving messages. This is called a *starving consumer.*

194

Have in mind that the number of active consumers will depend on the number of partitions currently available for that topic. In cases where brokers fail, we may enter in a scenario where we don't have a leader for a particular partition.

If you need to increase the overall performance, remember that you can add more partitions to a topic later.

There are other client configurations you may use to increase the consumer processing capacity, like `consumersCount` and `consumerStreams`.

The `consumerStreams` parameter is responsible for setting the number of threads for the component's thread pool and the `consumersCount` is responsible for setting the number of Kafka consumers in the application. Every offset reading will be done in a single thread, which means that the number of concurrent readings you can do will depend on the number of consumers you have and if you have threads available for that consumer.

To illustrate this configuration, open the `camel-kafka-consumer-v2` project on your IDE. Let's see this project route so you can understand how this test works; look at Listing 5-8.

Listing 5-8. KafkaConsumerRoute.java File

```
public class KafkaConsumerRoute extends RouteBuilder {

@Override
public void configure() throws Exception {

from("{{kafka.uri}}")
 .routeId("consumer-route")
 .log("Headers : ${headers}")
 .log("Body : ${body}")
```

195

```
.process(new Processor() {
   @Override
 public void process(Exchange exchange) throws Exception {
  log.info("My thread is :"+Thread.currentThread().getName());
  log.info("Going to sleep...");
  Thread.sleep(10000);
    }
  });
}}
```

The only thing new on this route is that now you have a processor that puts the executing thread to sleep for ten seconds. This will help you to visualize the execution.

Let's look at the properties file in Listing 5-9.

Listing 5-9. camel-kafka-consumer-v2 properties File

```
topic=example1
brokers=localhost:9092
kafka.uri=kafka:{{topic}}?brokers={{brokers}}&clientId=${kaf
ka.clientid}&groupId=${kafka.groupid}&consumersCount=${kafka.
consumers.count}&consumerStreams=${kafka.consumers.stream}
```

Here you add the consumersCount and consumerStreams parameters, but you will also get them from the JVM properties.

To start testing this code, stop any running consumer. In a terminal, start the application like this:

```
camel-kafka-consumer-v2/ $ mvn clean quarkus:dev \
-Ddebug=5006 -Dkafka.clientid=test -Dkafka.groupid=testGroup \
-Dkafka.consumers.count=1 -Dkafka.consumers.stream=10
```

Here you are setting the parameters with their default values. To test how the application consumes the messages, run the following command in another terminal:

```
$ i=0; while [ $i -lt 3 ]; do ((i++));  curl -w "\n"  -X POST
'http://localhost:8080/kafka' -H 'Content-Type: text/plain'
-d "Message number: $i" ; done
```

Three messages are enough to show you that every ten seconds a single message will be processed, even though you have ten threads in the pool.

Now try with two Kafka consumers and the same amount of threads in the pool. Stop the consumer and start it again like this:

```
camel-kafka-consumer-v2/ $ mvn clean quarkus:dev
\              -Ddebug=5006 -Dkafka.clientid=test -Dkafka.
groupid=testGroup \
-Dkafka.consumers.count=2  Dkafka.consumers.stream=10
```

Now, instead of sending only three messages, send eight.

```
$ i=0; while [ $i -lt 8 ]; do ((i++));  curl -w "\n"  -X POST
'http://localhost:8080/kafka' -H 'Content-Type: text/plain'
-d "Message number: $i" ; done
```

You will see the application consuming two messages every ten seconds. But what happens if you have more consumers than threads? Stop the consumer application and start it like this:

```
camel-kafka-consumer-v2/ $ mvn clean quarkus:dev \
-Ddebug=5006 -Dkafka.clientid=test -Dkafka.groupid=testGroup
\              -Dkafka.consumers.count=2  -Dkafka.consumers.
stream=1
```

Send three messages again. You will see that only one message is processed every ten seconds.

What you did here were ways to scale the consumer vertically, by allowing it to consume more resources, in this case assignments to partitions. When you scale an application vertically you also need to adjust how the application consumes computational resources like memory and CPU.

You are following a microservice approach for the applications, so you don't want them to become so big that they might hurt other important microservices characteristics like agility in a graceful shutdown or the capacity to scale horizontally (by adding new instances). It's all a matter of knowing your data and knowing your application, and then adjusting the configuration properly. Testing is a must.

Offset Reset

You may add new consumers for existing topics that may already have messages on them. In this case, you need to set the right behavior for your new consumer.

Before discussing what you can do when a topic already has messages, I need you to take a look at something. With the broker running, run the following command on a terminal:

```
$ docker exec -it broker /opt/kafka/bin/kafka-topics.sh
                --bootstrap-server localhost:9092 --list
```

This command lists the topic available in the broker. If you didn't delete any topic, your output should be like Figure 5-13.

```
gcamposo:~ $ docker exec -it broker /opt/kafka/bin/kafka-topics.sh
--bootstrap-server localhost:9092 --list
__consumer_offsets
example1
myTestTopic
```

Figure 5-13. *Topic list*

Each partition offset consumed by a group id is saved in the
__consumer_offsets topic. You saw in the application logs that in every
startup process the client would check which offset was available for a
given partition, always looking for the latest reference.

Before starting this new example, you need a fresh topic. Let's clean
your old topics. Stop any running application and run the following
command to do so:

```
$ docker exec -it broker /opt/kafka/bin/kafka-topics.sh
       --bootstrap-server localhost:9092 --delete --topic
       myTestTopic
```

```
$ docker exec -it broker /opt/kafka/bin/kafka-topics.sh
       --bootstrap-server localhost:9092 --delete --topic
       example1
```

To start your test, you will need a topic, but this time instead of creating
one yourself, you will let the topic auto-creation do it. It will create by
default a topic with a single replica and a single partition. That will be
enough for your test.

If this is not a desirable configuration, you can disable the auto
creation by setting the auto.create.topics.enable property
to false in the server.properties file in Kafka's config directory.
This will require a broker restart.

Run the camel-kafka-producer application again. Once it starts, send
ten messages using the following command:

```
$ i=0; while [ $i -lt 10 ]; do ((i++));  curl -w "\n"  -X POST
'http://localhost:8080/kafka' -H 'Content-Type: text/plain'
-d "Message number: $i" ; done
```

You can now start the consumer knowing that there are messages in the topic. Start the `camel-kafka-consumer` application like this:

```
camel-kafka-consumer/ $ mvn clean quarkus:dev -Ddebug=5006
    -Dkafka.clientid=test -Dkafka.groupid=testGroup
```

You didn't get any message, did you? Well, that is the expected behavior. By default the component property for auto offset reset is set to take the latest offset in the partition. Look at the logs in the consumer application, shown in Listing 5-10.

Listing 5-10. camel-kafka-consumer Application Log Snippet

```
2021-06-06 20:52:09,669 INFO [org.apa.kaf.cli.con.
int.ConsumerCoordinator] (Camel (camel-1) thread #0 -
KafkaConsumer[example1]) [Consumer clientId=test,
groupId=testGroup] Found no committed offset for partition
example1-0

2021-06-06 20:52:09,693 INFO [org.apa.kaf.cli.con.
int.SubscriptionState] (Camel (camel-1) thread #0 -
KafkaConsumer[example1]) [Consumer clientId=test,
groupId=testGroup] Resetting offset for partition example1-0 to
position FetchPosition{offset=10, offsetEpoch=Optional.empty,
currentLeader=LeaderAndEpoch{leader=Optional[localhost:9092
(id: 1001 rack: null)], epoch=0}}.
```

The first log shows that no committed offset for partition `example1-0` was found for the provided group id. The second one shows that the offset was reset for `FetchPosition offset=10`, which will be the next offset generated.

Send a single message to check the record header in the consumer log:

```
$ curl -w "\n"  -X POST 'http://localhost:8080/kafka'
-H 'Content-Type: text/plain'   -d "Single message"
```

In the logs you will find an entry like this:

```
2021-06-06 20:57:16,338 INFO  [consumer-route] (Camel (camel-1)
thread #0 - KafkaConsumer[example1]) Headers : {kafka.
HEADERS=RecordHeaders(headers = [], isReadOnly = false), kafka.
OFFSET=10, kafka.PARTITION=0, kafka.TIMESTAMP=1623023836299,
kafka.TOPIC=example1}
```

You can see that message offset is 10, which was the position marked in the consumer startup, but still you didn't get the previous messages. This can be a desired situation, since the new application may not want old messages. If you want to replay every message you have in a topic, you just need a new group id and the following configuration.

First, stop the consumer application. Change the kafka.uri property to look like this:

```
kafka.uri=kafka:{{topic}}?brokers={{brokers}}&clientId=${kafka.
clientid}&groupId=${kafka.groupid}&autoOffsetReset=earliest
```

Now, start the application like this:

```
camel-kafka-consumer/ $ mvn clean quarkus:dev
-Ddebug=5006    -Dkafka.clientid=test -Dkafka.groupid=newGroup
```

This way the application will get all the messages present in the topic and if you restart the application with the same parameters it won't get the same messages because the provided group id already has an offset saved and the client won't need to reset it.

Unit Testing Applications

To unit test applications, it is essential to keep code quality and make maintenance easier. When dealing with integration you may be interfacing with applications that are not straightforward to mock, like a message broker. Camel provides components and functionalities that can help you with this task.

For this new example, there's a new project called camel-kafka-tests. This project is a fusion between the camel-kafka-producer and camel-kafka-consumer plus unit tests.

It has a RouteBuilder to expose a REST interface and publish a message into a topic and a RouteBuilder to create a consumer for that topic. Let's start with the producer route in Listing 5-11.

Listing 5-11. RestKafkaRoute.java File

```
public class RestKafkaRoute extends RouteBuilder {

@Override
public void configure() throws Exception {

  rest("/kafka")
  .consumes(TEXT_PLAIN)
  .produces(TEXT_PLAIN)
  .post()
  .route()
    .routeId("rest-route")
    .log("sending message.")
    .removeHeaders("*")
    .to("{{kafka.uri.to}}")
    .removeHeaders("*")
    .setBody(constant("message sent."))
```

```
    .log("${body}")
  .endRest();

}
}
```

This route is essentially the one you have been using to publish messages in the topics. The only difference is that now the property name is a little less generic because now you have two routes. Let's look at the consumer in Listing 5-12.

Listing 5-12. KafkaConsumerRoute.java File

```
public class KafkaConsumerRoute extends RouteBuilder {

    @Override
    public void configure() throws Exception {

        from("{{kafka.uri.from}}")
        .routeId("consumer-route")
        .log("Headers : ${headers}")
        .to("{{final.endpoint}}");

    }
}
```

The only thing that changed in this one is the last step. Instead of logging using the log() DSL, you are going to use the log endpoint. You will see why in a minute.

In order to test this code, you need to create the topic first. Run

```
$ docker exec -it broker /opt/kafka/bin/kafka-topics.sh
\      --create --bootstrap-server localhost:9092
\                --replication-factor 1 --partitions 2 --topic
                example2
```

You can then start the application:

```
camel-kafka-tests/ $ mvn quarkus:dev
```

And send messages to test:

```
$ curl -X POST 'http://localhost:8080/kafka' \
-H 'Content-Type: text/plain' -d "hi"
```

Now that you have seen how the application works, you can start focusing on the unit test. Observe the new additions to the project's pom, shown in Listing 5-13.

Listing 5-13. camel-kafka-tests pom.xml File Snippet

```
...
    <dependency>
    <groupId>org.apache.camel.quarkus</groupId>
    <artifactId>camel-quarkus-log</artifactId>
    </dependency>
    <dependency>
    <groupId>org.apache.camel.quarkus</groupId>
    <artifactId>camel-quarkus-direct</artifactId>
    <scope>test</scope>
    </dependency>
    <dependency>
    <groupId>org.apache.camel.quarkus</groupId>
    <artifactId>camel-quarkus-mock</artifactId>
    <scope>test</scope>
    </dependency>
    <dependency>
    <groupId>io.quarkus</groupId>
    <artifactId>quarkus-junit5</artifactId>
```

```
<scope>test</scope>
</dependency>
<dependency>
<groupId>io.rest-assured</groupId>
<artifactId>rest-assured</artifactId>
<scope>test</scope>
</dependency>
```

...

I'm only highlighting the new additions for this example.

You already know camel-quarkus-log. You are using it because you are also logging using the component. You are going to use camel-quarkus-direct and camel-quarkus-mock to substitute and mock some endpoint definitions. This will give you flexibility to perform the unit test without having a running Kafka broker. The Quarkus implementation for JUnit 5 is the base for the tests. It will set up the environment properly, taking into account the Quarkus building model. And last you have REST Assured, a popular library for testing REST applications.

So let's take a look at the first unit test class, shown in Listing 5-14.

Listing 5-14. RestKafkaRouteTest.java File

```
@QuarkusTest
public class RestKafkaRouteTest {

    @Test
    public void test() {

        given()
            .contentType(ContentType.TEXT)
            .body("Hello")
        .when()
            .post("/kafka")
```

```
        .then()
            .statusCode(200)
            .body(is("message sent."));

    }
}
```

You start by annotating the test class with @QuarkusTest. This will allow the JUnit implementation to start the application and the Camel context within. The test is pretty simple. You are using REST Assured to send a message to the REST endpoint and then assert if the response status code is 200 and the response message is "message sent."

You may ask about the Kafka endpoint call in the middle of the route. That call was mocked. Take a look at the application.properties files under the test folder, as shown in Listing 5-15.

Listing 5-15. application.properties for Test

```
kafka.uri.to=mock:kafka-topic
kafka.uri.from=direct:topic
final.endpoint=mock:destination
```

In this example, you declare endpoints using properties, so you can substitute the properties' values when testing. This way you can still unit test the routing logic without having to provide a broker during test time. In this test, the mock component is used to pass the exchange on, without any modification. Then the routing finishes and the HTTP client will get a response.

Now let's see the consumer route, in Listing 5-16.

Listing 5-16. KafkaConsumerRouteTest.java File

```java
@QuarkusTest
public class KafkaConsumerRouteTest {

    @Inject
    CamelContext camelContext;

    @Inject
    ProducerTemplate producerTemplate;

    @ConfigProperty(name = "kafka.uri.from")
    String direct;

    @ConfigProperty(name = "final.endpoint")
    String mock;

    private static final String MSG = "Hello";

    @Test
    public void test() throws InterruptedException {

        producerTemplate.sendBody(direct, MSG);

        MockEndpoint mockEndpoint =
            camelContext.getEndpoint(mock, MockEndpoint.class);
        mockEndpoint.expectedMessageCount(1);
        mockEndpoint.assertIsSatisfied();

        assertEquals(MSG,mockEndpoint.getExchanges().get(0)
                            .getMessage().getBody())

    }
}
```

Here you use a different approach to test routes because your route consumer must be mocked. Since you don't have a broker running, it's necessary to substitute the Kafka component for the direct component. This way you can invoke the route using a `ProducerTemplate`, which will essentially create one exchange and send it to the direct endpoint. From there the route logic will proceed. The problem with this route is that it doesn't do much, which is why you change the last step to use `to()`. In the unit test, you replace the log definition for the mock component and use it to check the route status. By injecting the Camel context, you can get endpoint references. Here you get the reference to the mock endpoint. This endpoint will retain information of the exchanges it received, and using that information you can assert if the route performed as expected. You can check how many messages were received and if the message body is the same as you sent, since no processing should have been made.

To execute these tests, run the following command:

```
camel-kafka-tests/ $ mvn clean test
```

Expect to receive the following messages in the logs:

```
[INFO] Results:
[INFO]
[INFO] Tests run: 2, Failures: 0, Errors: 0, Skipped: 0
[INFO]
[INFO] ------------------------------------------------------------
[INFO] BUILD SUCCESS
[INFO] ------------------------------------------------------------
```

The techniques shown here can be used to set many different test scenarios. You could, for example, substitute endpoint definitions with bean calls and use those methods to inject any object you can mock in the exchange. This way you can virtually mock every integration you need to do. Just remember to keep your routing logic clean and use properties to declare endpoints, and unit testing Camel will be easy.

Summary

This chapter was dedicated to asynchronous communication between services and the most common way to do it is using message-oriented middleware. You learned about the following topics in this chapter:

- Characteristics of message-oriented middleware

- The importance of asynchronous communication for robust architecture

- Kafka's concepts and architecture

- How to run and perform basic configurations with Kafka

- How to set up Camel to access Kafka topics

- How to perform unit tests using Quarkus and Camel

In the next and final chapter, we dive into how to run these called cloud native applications in a Kubernetes environment and the implications of this approach for architecture designs.

CHAPTER 6

Deploying Applications to Kubernetes

Welcome to the last part of your journey towards cloud native integration. So far, you have been focusing on how to do integration, learning Camel's concepts, and applying components for different use cases, but now you will focus on how to deploy those applications in a cloud native way using Kubernetes.

Decisions made earlier will have a huge impact on the experience of developing applications for Kubernetes and the biggest one is the use of Quarkus. Since it is not required for you to run Camel integrations; it's a choice between other frameworks or simply running Camel's Main class. Quarkus is the perfect choice for what you are aiming for because it was made to be cloud native. That is something that Camel itself wasn't originally made to be, as the concept didn't exist back then when it was created, although, thanks to its robust architecture, it fits perfectly well in this type of setting.

I talked a lot about Java specifications and how they evolved to become adherent to cloud native principles. Those principles were developed and molded thanks to uncountable amounts of hours of people working to make reliable, resilient, and scalable services for the cloud, or in the cloud, and sharing their practices on open forums and open communities.

© Guilherme Camposo 2021
G. Camposo, *Cloud Native Integration with Apache Camel*,
https://doi.org/10.1007/978-1-4842-7211-4_6

One initiative that powerfully synthesizes best practices of cloud service development is the 12 Factor App, an open-source methodology initially made by developers at Heroku, a platform-as-a-service company. Those 12 rules define methods that are intrinsic to Kubernetes applications and how Quarkus was designed to be, so I strongly recommend you, in case you haven't yet, visit `https://12factor.net/` to get a more theoretical view on what you are executing here.

In this chapter, you will get an overview of what Kubernetes is and how it works. You will learn how to use minikube, a community tool used to experiment with Kubernetes locally and how to use Quarkus extensions to facilitate the process of working and deploying containers.

Without further delay, let's dive into the new topic.

Kubernetes

Kubernetes has become the standard for managing applications at scale. The biggest players in technology have converged in this open-source project, creating a series of products and services that provide support for this kind of platform or offering the platform itself. Let's understand what makes this project so relevant for organizations today.

In the digital era we are living in, scalability has become a fundamental characteristic in any service or solution adopted by organizations. We must expect that at any given time the demand for our services will increase either by the overall popularity of the product/service in the market, a pick of access, or we start to handle more data than we initially planned for. To scale is not enough; we also must maintain the same quality of service (response time, success rate, and so on).

Kubernetes fits perfectly in this highly demanding world for two simple reasons. The first one is that it works with containers, which is a language/product-agnostic way to pack and distribute applications and a more efficient way to utilize machine resources to host applications.

The second one is that it provides all the automation required to manage containers in various scenarios at scale, as a highly available solution.

You have been using containers to interact with applications such as Keycloak and Kafka, but you also used a container to run a Camel route in Chapter 1. At this point, you already have a good grasp of what containers mean and what kind of benefits they offer. Let's focus on Kubernetes, how it works, and what types of automations it offers, starting with its high-level architecture. Look at Figure 6-1. Every box represents a hosting machine.

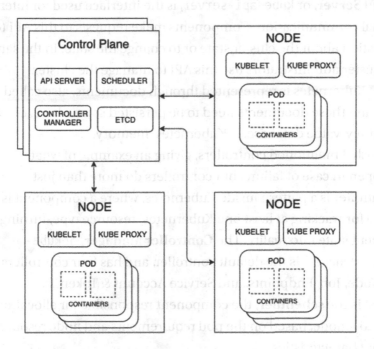

Figure 6-1. *Kubernetes high level architecture*

Containers are abstracted into entities called **pods**. A pod is a composition of one or more containers and the necessary configuration to run those containers. This structure is what Kubernetes really orchestrates. Pods are distributed between running nodes in the cluster and that is why you can achieve high availability. If a node fails, there are controllers in place to guarantee that you have the desired number of pods running in the cluster. The controller will try to allocate the pods present in the failing node in another available node to keep the state consistent.

Talking about the hosts, the **control plane** is the brain behind the cluster automation. It is responsible for the orchestration of pods and cluster members. In a normally found high available setup, you will find it in a group of three or more hosts. There are four main components present in a control plane instance. Let's see them one by one.

The **API Server**, or kube-api-server, is the interface used for internal and external communication. Components make requests to this API to get information about the cluster state or to change the state. In the same way, the cluster administrators use this API to manage the cluster.

State in Kubernetes is represented through documents, also called resources, and these documents need to be persisted somewhere. ETCD, a distributed key-value database, is Kubernetes' memory.

Previously I mentioned controllers, giving an example of what would happen in case of failure, but controllers do more than just that. A controller is a pattern inside Kubernetes, where a component is responsible for tracking at least one Kubernetes' resource type, turning the document state into reality. The **Controller Manager**, or kube-controller-manager, is the default controller, and has four controllers inside it: Node, Job, Endpoints, and Service Account & Token.

And last is the **scheduler**, the component responsible for allocating a new pod to a node, based on the pod requirements and node resources available or characteristics.

There are important components in the nodes too. The first one is the **Kubelet** agent. It is responsible for handling and checking the health of containers described in PodSpecs. If the control plane is the brain, this component could easily be considered the hands.

The second component is the **kube-proxy**. One thing that I didn't discuss yet is how this level of automation is possible. Creating pods on the fly and moving them around sounds good, but how does this work with

214

the network? Port and IP assignment, and possibly load balance for scaled services, are tasks that need to be automated. Kube-proxy is part of the explanation of how it works. It is a network proxy that runs on each node in the cluster. It maintains network rules that allow network communication to pods from network sessions inside or outside of the cluster.

Another node component that is listed in the Kubernetes documentation is the container runtime. Docker is an example of a container runtime. I'm not listing it here because there are some Kubernetes-based products that run the components present in the control plane in containers. In this case, both the nodes and control plane would have the container runtime, turning the runtime into a common need. Therefore, I am not describing it as a node component.

We are just scratching the surface on Kubernetes. Before you go deeper in how it works and what configurations can be done, you need to start with something practical. In the next section, you will see how to experiment with Kubernetes in a personal computer set up.

Minikube

I don't expect you to have a cluster in your house or to have access to a cluster in the public cloud. There are easier ways to study and experiment with Kubernetes. Let's try minikube.

minikube is a tool that enables you to create a local Kubernetes "cluster". You will be able to apply the same configurations you would do for an application in a cluster but using a single node to do it. This way you will have the experience of what it is like to configure an application and how it would work, without really having a cluster.

Visit the minikube website, `https://minikube.sigs.k8s.io/`, for instructions on how to install it on the operating system you are using. I used Minikube version v1.20.0.

You also need **kubectl**. This command line tool will allow you to communicate with the Kubernetes API. You can get it from the Kubernetes project website, `https://kubernetes.io/docs/tasks/tools/`, or you can use the kubectl present in the minikube CLI, like this:

```
$ minikube kubectl help
```

Once you have installed the binaries properly, start minikube with the following command:

```
$ minikube start
```

You may want to use options such as `--cpus` or `--memory` to increase the instance capacity. Just take into consideration the amount of available resources you have. I will use the default values for the examples.

To test if minikube is responding, run the following command:

```
$ kubectl get pods -A
```

This command will return which pods are running, as in Figure 6-2.

```
~ $ kubectl get pods -A
NAMESPACE     NAME                                   READY   STATUS    RESTARTS   AGE
kube-system   coredns-74ff55c5b-fpxm9                1/1     Running   0          68s
kube-system   etcd-minikube                          0/1     Running   0          81s
kube-system   kube-apiserver-minikube                1/1     Running   0          81s
kube-system   kube-controller-manager-minikube       0/1     Running   0          81s
kube-system   kube-proxy-v9lm7                        1/1     Running   0          68s
kube-system   kube-scheduler-minikube                1/1     Running   0          81s
kube-system   storage-provisioner                    1/1     Running   0          81s
```

Figure 6-2. *GET pods*

You may already recognize some of the pods. They are the components I mentioned earlier, but since you only have a single host, you have in this host the control plane and node's components.

I didn't mention earlier the **coredns** component, which is a default component but is considered an add-on. This component is responsible for providing a DNS server, which serves DNS records for the Kubernetes services.

The storage-provisioner is a component provided by minikube to allow us to use persistence in our pods but is not something you will need for the examples.

Another important thing to observe in that image is the first column called **namespace**. It is an abstraction used by Kubernetes to create separation between resources. This way you can isolate resources as if they were in different environments, like production and development.

In the command, you use the option -A, which means that you want to retrieve pods from all namespaces. In this case, it helped you to identify if there were running pods, because you didn't know which namespace you had.

Before you move on to the next section, delete the minikube installation. You will need a different one for the next section. Stop it by running the following command:

```
$ minikube stop
```

And then delete it using the following command:

```
$ minikube delete
```

First Application Deployment

You saw how to create a local Kubernetes and learned more concepts about it. To move forward, you need to learn how to actually deploy an application and how to interact with it.

217

When you used containers in the previous chapters, you relied on the Docker Hub and local registry to retrieve images from. With Kubernetes, it is the same thing. It also needs a registry reachable by the cluster to be able to get the images and run the container. In this case, you need to provide a container registry for minikube.

Start by creating a new minikube instance like this:

```
$ minikube start --insecure-registry "10.0.0.0/24"
```

Since you won't provide a secured registry for this installation, you need to configure the instance to allow insecure registries from inside of minikube.

Once your instance has started, you can add a registry to it running this command:

```
$ minikube addons enable registry
```

minikube will download and run the registry image. After it finishes, you can check if the registry is running using this command:

```
$ kubectl get pods -n kube-system
```

You are using -n to define in which namespace you want to perform your query. You should get a response similar to Figure 6-3.

```
~ $ kubectl get pods -n kube-system
NAME                                  READY   STATUS    RESTARTS   AGE
coredns-74ff55c5b-pmrhd               1/1     Running   0          45s
etcd-minikube                         0/1     Running   0          59s
kube-apiserver-minikube               1/1     Running   0          59s
kube-controller-manager-minikube      0/1     Running   0          59s
kube-proxy-f94f5                      1/1     Running   0          45s
kube-scheduler-minikube               1/1     Running   0          59s
registry-proxy-s2rmh                  1/1     Running   0          44s
registry-t8hnc                        1/1     Running   0          45s
storage-provisioner                   1/1     Running   0          58s
```

Figure 6-3. *Registry pods*

Kubernetes has a resource called **service**. This resource creates a DNS record to allow pods to access other pods by name. This is important because pods can scale and move to different nodes in the cluster, changing its address, but client applications only need the service name to reach the application. This resource, besides creating a predictable name to be used by other pods, also adds the possibility of load balance requests to different pods or pods with more than one instance. When the registry was installed, a service was created. Check the services available in the installation with this command:

```
$ kubectl get service -n kube-system
```

This will give you the list of services in the kube-system namespace, like Figure 6-4.

```
~ $ kubectl get service -n kube-system
NAME        TYPE        CLUSTER-IP        EXTERNAL-IP    PORT(S)                    AGE
kube-dns    ClusterIP   10.96.0.10        <none>         53/UDP,53/TCP,9153/TCP     5m57s
registry    ClusterIP   10.104.150.175    <none>         80/TCP,443/TCP             5m45s
```

Figure 6-4. *GET service kube-system*

The registry service is a ClusterIP type of service, which means it will have an IP resolvable inside minikube's network. If you want to get more details about this service, you can make a more precise query like this:

```
$ kubectl get service registry -o json -n kube-system
```

This command will return something similar to Listing 6-1.

Listing 6-1. Service Resource

```
{
    "apiVersion": "v1",
    "kind": "Service",
    "metadata": {
        "annotations": {
```

```
        "kubectl.kubernetes.io/last-applied-configuration": "..."
    },
    "creationTimestamp": "2021-06-13T11:00:49Z",
    "labels": {
        "addonmanager.kubernetes.io/mode": "Reconcile",
        "kubernetes.io/minikube-addons": "registry"
    },
    "name": "registry",
    "namespace": "kube-system",
    "resourceVersion": "467",
    "uid": "2f31047f-8ae5-4920-bc4d-9a84ad39288f"
},
"spec": {
    "clusterIP": "10.103.159.51",
    "clusterIPs": [
        "10.103.159.51"
    ],
    "ports": [
        {
            "name": "http",
            "port": 80,
            "protocol": "TCP",
            "targetPort": 5000
        },
        {
            "name": "https",
            "port": 443,
            "protocol": "TCP",
            "targetPort": 443
        }
```

```
    ],
    "selector": {
        "actual-registry": "true",
        "kubernetes.io/minikube-addons": "registry"
    },
    "sessionAffinity": "None",
    "type": "ClusterIP"
  },
  "status": {
      "loadBalancer": {}
  }
}
```

As I said, the resources in Kubernetes are documents, and those documents can be represented in YAML or JSON files. Here I used JSON because I want you to retrieve a specific value from its specification and you are going to use jsonpath to get it.

The Kubernetes DNS configuration is not used by minikube's virtual machine, but you need the Docker used by minikube to be able to resolve the registry host to run the image. So, let's create a workaround solution for this.

First, let's retrieve the service IP. You will use jsonpath to customize the query result, bringing back only the ClusterIP value. Use the following command:

```
$ kubectl get service registry -o=jsonpath='{.spec.clusterIP}'
-n kube-system
```

You will use this command later. Now you need an application to be deployed. Let's use the camel-hello-minikube project.

Open the project in your IDE. Observe the project's route in Listing 6-2.

Listing 6-2. HelloMinikubeRoute.java

```java
public class HelloMinikubeRoute extends RouteBuilder {
    @Override
    public void configure() throws Exception {

      rest("/helloMinikube")
      .get()
          .route()
          .routeId("k8s-hello-minikube")
          .log("Request Received.")
          .setBody(constant("Hello from minikube."))
      .endRest();

    }
}
```

This is a simple "Hello World" type of application, just to demonstrate how to deploy Camel applications into minikube. In this project, you are using the `quarkus-container-image-jib` as you did in the first chapter. You will use this extension to build the container image and push it to the created registry.

In order to be able to push images to the registry, you need to access it from outside minikube's network. You can enable this using a `kubectl` command called `port-forward`.

In a separate terminal window or tab, run the following command:

```
$ kubectl port-forward service/registry -n kube-system 5000:80
```

This command will create a tunnel from your local network to the Kubernetes cluster. After you run it, the terminal will be hanging, waiting for connections. Let it stay open.

Now that you can connect to the registry, let's build the application and push the image. On a separate terminal window, go to the camel-hello-minikube directory. From there run this command:

```
camel-hello-minikube $ mvn clean package \
-Dquarkus.container-image.push=true \
-Dquarkus.container-image.build=true \
-Dquarkus.container-image.group=apress \
-Dquarkus.container-image.registry=localhost:5000 \
-Dquarkus.container-image.insecure=true
```

New parameters are being used here. First, you inform the extension that you want to push the image to a registry by setting quarkus.container-image.push=true and informing the registry address in quarkus.container-image.registry=localhost:5000. This registry is not secure, which is why you need to set quarkus.container-image.insecure=true.

Once the Maven build has finished, you can check if the image is available in the registry by running this command:

```
$ curl http://localhost:5000/v2/_catalog
```

The response should be like Figure 6-5.

```
~ $ curl http://localhost:5000/v2/_catalog
{"repositories":["apress/camel-hello-minikube"]}
```

Figure 6-5. *Registry catalog*

You can stop the port-forward now.

Going back to the project and inside the k8s folder, open the deployment.yml file shown in Listing 6-3.

Listing 6-3. Camel-hello-minikube Deployment File

```
apiVersion: apps/v1
kind: Deployment
metadata:
  labels:
    app: camel-hello-minikube
  name: camel-hello-minikube
  namespace: first-deploy
spec:
  replicas: 1
  selector:
    matchLabels:
      app: camel-hello-minikube
  strategy:
    type: RollingUpdate
  template:
    metadata:
      labels:
        app: camel-hello-minikube
    spec:
      containers:
        - image: {REGISTRY}/apress/camel-hello-minikube:1.0.0
          imagePullPolicy: IfNotPresent
          name: camel-hello-minikube
          ports:
            - containerPort: 8080
              protocol: TCP
```

As I said, the resources in Kubernetes are documents, and the deployment descriptor is no different. Here you have a minimal deployment configuration file. You set the container image, the number of pod replicas, how the deployment should roll out, and labels that make it possible to identify the components of this deployment resource.

You must have noticed the {REGISTRY} marker. You need to substitute this value to be able to create this resource in minikube.

First, let's create a namespace to host the deployment. Use this command:

```
$ kubectl create namespace first-deploy
```

Use sed, a stream editor, to dynamically replace the marker and create the resource. In the project directory, run this command:

```
camel-hello-minikube $ sed "s/{REGISTRY}/$(kubectl get svc
registry -o=jsonpath='{.spec.clusterIP}' -n kube-system)/" k8s/
deployment.yml | kubectl create -f -
```

You didn't need to pass the namespace in the create command because the namespace was already declared in the resource file.

The command above uses the abbreviated version of the resource name. Instead of service it used svc. Most of Kubernetes fundamental resources have an abbreviation.

You can check the deployment process by looking at the events generated in the namespace using this command:

```
$ kubectl get events -n first-deploy
```

You may also check the state of deployments in the namespace. Run this command to see if the pod is ready:

```
$ kubectl get deployment -n first-deploy
```

If everything went well, your result should look like Figure 6-6.

```
~ $ kubectl get deployment -n first-deploy
NAME                    READY   UP-TO-DATE   AVAILABLE    AGE
camel-hello-minikube    1/1     1            1            29s
```

Figure 6-6. *GET deployment*

Having a 1/1 ready means that one pod of the one required is running without perceivable errors. I'm saying "perceivable errors" because the application may be running but not functioning properly. If you want to be more assertive about this status line, you should implement better health checks in the application. We will talk more about this in the next sections.

I want you to be aware of what a deployment resource looks like, which is why you used a file to create the deployment, but there is another way to create a default deployment using the kubectl. You could have used this command:

```
$ kubectl create deployment camel-hello-minikube
--image=$(kubectl get svc registry -n kube-system
-o=jsonpath='{.spec.clusterIP}')/apress/camel-hello-
minikube:1.0.0 --port=8080 -n first-deploy
```

To access and test this deployment you need to run port-forward again. First, let's create a service for this deployment. In a terminal window, run

```
$ kubectl expose deployment camel-hello-minikube -n first-
deploy
```

This will create a ClusterIP type of service for you, targeting the only declared port. You can check the result by running

```
$ kubectl get services -n first-deploy
```

Now you can use this service to create the tunnel with port-forward:

```
$ kubectl port-forward service/camel-hello-minikube \
-n first-deploy 8080:8080
```

You do not need a service to port-forward to a pod. I'm only using this approach here so you don't need to look for the pod's name and to demonstrate how to expose a deployment.

In another terminal, you may test the application using cURL:

```
$ curl http://localhost:8080/helloMinikube
```

You should get a response like Figure 6-7.

```
~ $ curl -w '\n' http://localhost:8080/helloMinikube
Hello from minikube.
```

Figure 6-7. *cURL response*

Also, check the container log. It will help you to understand how the application is behaving in minikube.

```
$ kubectl logs deployment/camel-hello-minikube -c camel-hello-minikube -n first-deploy
```

Once you are done testing the example, you may want to delete what was created to save resources for other tests. You can delete a namespace and every resource in it by running a command like this:

```
$ kubectl delete namespace first-deploy
```

Quarkus-minikube

In the previous section I wanted to introduce you to a few concepts and possibilities when using minikube and Quarkus extensions. You saw how to push images to external registries and how to use port-forward to access applications inside minikube, but there are easier ways to do this depending on what you are trying to achieve. In this section, you will see how the quarkus-minikube extension can help you when testing with minikube.

Before starting this new example, let's get a brand new minikube instance. Run the following commands in sequence:

```
$ minikube stop
$ minikube delete
$ minikube start
```

The first thing to notice is that you are not setting --insecure because you are not going to use a container registry. Instead you are going to save the image straight in minikube's Docker registry. You are going to use the same project, camel-hello-minikube, but you need to add a new extension to it.

Under the camel-hello-minikube directory, run this command:

```
camel-hello-minikube $ mvn quarkus:add-extension \
  -Dextensions="quarkus-minikube"
```

This extension generates Kubernetes manifests (minikube.yaml and minikube.json) that will be used to deploy the application. When used with quarkus-container-image-jib, jib will push the image to Minikube's Docker and quarkus-minikube will apply the deployment and service resources in the manifest to minikube.

Before building and running those extensions, you need minikube's Docker configuration. Run the following command to expose the configuration:

```
$ minikube -p minikube docker-env
```

You will get a return similar to Figure 6-8.

```
~ $ minikube -p minikube docker-env
export DOCKER_TLS_VERIFY="1"
export DOCKER_HOST="tcp://192.168.64.14:2376"
export DOCKER_CERT_PATH="/Users/gcamposo/.minikube/certs"
export MINIKUBE_ACTIVE_DOCKERD="minikube"

# To point your shell to minikube's docker-daemon, run:
# eval $(minikube -p minikube docker-env)
```

Figure 6-8. *minikube's Docker configuration*

The value of the variable DOCKER_HOST is the minikube virtual machine IP address plus a port number. You can check the IP by running

```
$ minikube ip
```

Now that you know how to retrieve the configuration, you need to load it in the terminal session. This way when you run the Quarkus plugin, jib will know how to connect to the desired Docker.

Run this:

```
$ eval $(minikube -p minikube docker-env)
```

Let's create a new namespace for this application:

```
$ kubectl create namespace second-deploy
```

Change the kubectl context to point to this new namespace. The extension kubernetes-client will use this information to determine which cluster and namespace to send the created resources to. Run the following command to make the change:

```
$ kubectl config set-context --current --namespace=second-deploy
```

Then build the application like this:

```
camel-hello-minikube $ mvn clean package  \
-Dquarkus.container-image.group=apress \
-Dquarkus.kubernetes.deploy=true \
-Dquarkus.kubernetes.deployment-target=minikube
```

By setting quarkus.kubernetes.deploy=true the extensions will build the image and push the generated manifests to Kubernetes. In this case, you targeted Minikube using quarkus.kubernetes.deployment-target=minikube.

Go to target/kubernetes and look at the generated file, shown in Listing 6-4.

Listing 6-4. minikube.yaml

```
---
apiVersion: v1
kind: Service
metadata:
  annotations:
  labels:
    app.kubernetes.io/name: camel-hello-minikube
    app.kubernetes.io/version: 1.0.0
  name: camel-hello-minikube
spec:
  ports:
  - name: http
    nodePort: 30254
    port: 8080
    targetPort: 8080
```

```
    selector:
      app.kubernetes.io/name: camel-hello-minikube
      app.kubernetes.io/version: 1.0.0
    type: NodePort
---
apiVersion: apps/v1
kind: Deployment
metadata:
  annotations:
  labels:
    app.kubernetes.io/name: camel-hello-minikube
    app.kubernetes.io/version: 1.0.0
  name: camel-hello-minikube
spec:
  replicas: 1
  selector:
    matchLabels:
      app.kubernetes.io/name: camel-hello-minikube
      app.kubernetes.io/version: 1.0.0
  template:
    metadata:
      annotations:
      labels:
        app.kubernetes.io/name: camel-hello-minikube
        app.kubernetes.io/version: 1.0.0
    spec:
      containers:
      - env:
        - name: KUBERNETES_NAMESPACE
          valueFrom:
            fieldRef:
              fieldPath: metadata.namespace
```

```
image: apress/camel-hello-minikube:1.0.0
imagePullPolicy: IfNotPresent
name: camel-hello-minikube
ports:
- containerPort: 8080
  name: http
  protocol: TCP
```

As you can see, the service and deployment were generated. The service is configured as a NodePort type, which means it will expose a port in the minikube VM so you can access the application from outside the installation. The deployment is a standard one.

You will see in a future section how to add different parameters to this document.

You could use this plugin to only create the manifest by not setting quarkus.kubernetes.deploy. This way you could push the manifest yourself or use it as a template. One important thing to have in mind is that quarkus-minikube has some prerequisites:

- The image will be built by minikube's Docker.

- The application will be exposed using NodePort.

If these characteristics are not something you are expecting to create, you may use the quarkus-kubernetes extension to generate the manifests for you with more flexibility, but with more parameters required.

Check if the deployment was successfully created using this command:

```
$ kubectl get deployment -n second-deploy
```

Before testing the application, let's take a look at minikube's Docker. To access the virtual machine, use this command:

```
$ minikube ssh
```

Once you are in, you can use Docker commands to check how Docker is configured, for example, checking if the image you expected to be produced is there, like in Figure 6-9.

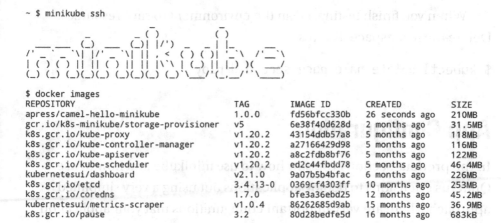

```
~ $ minikube ssh
```
```
$ docker images
REPOSITORY                                    TAG       IMAGE ID       CREATED         SIZE
apress/camel-hello-minikube                   1.0.0     fd56bfcc330b   26 seconds ago  210MB
gcr.io/k8s-minikube/storage-provisioner       v5        6e38f40d628d   2 months ago    31.5MB
k8s.gcr.io/kube-proxy                         v1.20.2   43154ddb57a8   5 months ago    118MB
k8s.gcr.io/kube-controller-manager            v1.20.2   a27166429d98   5 months ago    116MB
k8s.gcr.io/kube-apiserver                     v1.20.2   a8c2fdb8bf76   5 months ago    122MB
k8s.gcr.io/kube-scheduler                     v1.20.2   ed2c44fbdd78   5 months ago    46.4MB
kubernetesui/dashboard                        v2.1.0    9a07b5b4bfac   6 months ago    226MB
k8s.gcr.io/etcd                               3.4.13-0  0369cf4303ff   10 months ago   253MB
k8s.gcr.io/coredns                            1.7.0     bfe3a36ebd25   12 months ago   45.2MB
kubernetesui/metrics-scraper                  v1.0.4    86262685d9ab   15 months ago   36.9MB
k8s.gcr.io/pause                              3.2       80d28bedfe5d   16 months ago   683kB
```

Figure 6-9. minikube ssh session

You may close the session by typing exit and pressing Enter.

You know the extension provided a NodePort service for you based on what is in the manifest file, but there is another way to get this information more easily. Run the following command:

```
$ minikube service list
```

Observe Figure 6-10 to see the output. Remember that you probably are going to have different VM IP and port numbers.

```
~ $ minikube service list
|---------------|----------------------|----------------|----------------------------|
|   NAMESPACE   |         NAME         |  TARGET PORT   |            URL             |
|---------------|----------------------|----------------|----------------------------|
| default       | kubernetes           | No node port   |                            |
| kube-system   | kube-dns             | No node port   |                            |
| second-deploy | camel-hello-minikube | http/8080      | http://192.168.64.14:30254 |
|---------------|----------------------|----------------|----------------------------|
```

Figure 6-10. Service list

To test the application, just send a cURL request pointing to the exhibited URL (note that your IP could be slightly different), like this:

```
$ curl http://192.168.64.10:30254/helloMinikube
```

When you finish testing, clean the environment to save resources. Delete the namespace like this:

```
$ kubectl delete namespace second-deploy
```

App Configuration

In the previous sections you saw how to use minikube and how to use Quarkus extensions to deploy applications but using a very simplified approach. There are very important configurations that your application must have to be minimally considered production ready. We will discuss those.

Environment Variables

Containerized applications normally use environment variables to configure themselves during or before startup. Some images may use those values in startup scripts; some may use them directly in the application (as you are going to do), but what is important is that a single image can be used for different purposes or for different environments depending on the configuration passed to it. Let's see how to put the extensions and Camel together to enable this important feature.

As I mentioned when talking about Quarkus in the first chapter, it implements the MicroProfile Config specification. Well, it is not exactly Quarkus that implements it but the SmallRye Config project that is packed in it. This project allows you to retrieve configurations from five different sources:

- System properties

- Environment variables

- The .env file placed in the working directory

- An application.properties file placed in a directory
  called config, on the same level where the application
  runs

- An application.properties file packed with the
  application code

You already used system properties in the Kafka examples when setting
clientIds and groupId names, and you have been using application.
properties files packed with the code in the majority of the examples,
but now let's focus on using environment variables. This approach is
particularly interesting when using containers and Kubernetes, since you
can easily change its value when running an image.

You are going to use the camel-env-msg project for this example. Open
it in your IDE. Examine the project route in Listing 6-5.

Listing 6-5. EnvMSGRoute.java File

```java
public class EnvMSGRoute extends RouteBuilder {

    @Override
    public void configure() throws Exception {
        rest("/helloEnv")
        .get()
            .route()
            .routeId("env-msg")
            .log("Request Received")
            .setBody(constant("{{app.msg}}"))
```

```
    .endRest();

  }
}
```

This is another simple route example focused on showing you a
specific configuration in Camel and Quarkus. Here you have a REST route
that returns a message defined in a constant. The constant refers to a
property key called app.msg. Look at the application.properties file in
Listing 6-6.

Listing 6-6. Application.properties File

```
# Route properties
application.message=Default Message
app.msg=${application.message}

# Kubernetes configuration
quarkus.container-image.group=apress
quarkus.kubernetes.env.vars.application-message=Message from
ENV var
```

Starting with the application's route-related properties, you have two
values. The app.msg entry is used by the route to retrieve a value, but
this entry value is retrieved from another property called application.
message. The latter is resolved by the SmallRye implementation, so
you can use it to define a default value and also to be substituted by an
environment variable. The library will look for different patterns to find an
environment variable that is a match, but the most commonly used pattern
is uppercase words separated by an underscore (_).

The last segment is a property related to how you are going to generate
the deployment resource for this project. This property could be read like
this:

```
quarkus.kubernetes.env.vars.[KEY]=[VALUE]
```

One important thing to take notice of is the pattern used in the key declaration. It will generate an environment variable with the following conventions:

- It replaces each character that is neither alphanumeric nor an underscore with an underscore.

- It converts the name to uppercase.

A key such as `application-message` will become a variable named `APPLICATION_MESSAGE`.

Let's test the application locally before sending it to Minikube. In a terminal window, navigate to the `camel-env-msg` directory and start the application like this:

```
camel-env-msg $ mvn quarkus:dev
```

In another terminal window, send a request like this to test the application:

```
$ curl -w "\n" http://localhost:8080/helloEnv
```

You will get a response like Figure 6-11.

```
~ $ curl -w '\n' http://localhost:8080/helloEnv
Default Message
```

Figure 6-11. *HelloEnv response*

Stop the application. In the same terminal, declare an environment variable and then start the application:

```
camel-env-msg $ export APPLICATION_MESSAGE='new message'
camel-env-msg $ mvn quarkus:dev
```

Test the application again. This time your response should look like Figure 6-12.

```
~ $ curl -w '\n' http://localhost:8080/helloEnv
new message
```

Figure 6-12. *New helloEnv response*

You were able to change the application configuration by using an environment variable, but how will it look in a deployment resource?

Pack the application like this:

```
camel-env-msg $ mvn clean package \
-Dquarkus.kubernetes.deployment-target=minikube
```

Look at the `target/kubernetes` directory and open the `minikube.yaml` file, shown in Listing 6-7.

Listing 6-7. Minikube.yaml Deployment

```
---
apiVersion: apps/v1
kind: Deployment
metadata:
  annotations:
  labels:
    app.kubernetes.io/name: camel-env-msg
    app.kubernetes.io/version: 1.0.0
  name: camel-env-msg
spec:
  replicas: 1
  selector:
    matchLabels:
      app.kubernetes.io/name: camel-env-msg
      app.kubernetes.io/version: 1.0.0
```

```
template:
  metadata:
    annotations:
    labels:
      app.kubernetes.io/name: camel-env-msg
      app.kubernetes.io/version: 1.0.0
  spec:
    containers:
    - env:
      - name: KUBERNETES_NAMESPACE
        valueFrom:
          fieldRef:
            fieldPath: metadata.namespace
      - name: APPLICATION_MESSAGE
        value: Message from ENV var
      image: apress/camel-env-msg:1.0.0
      imagePullPolicy: IfNotPresent
      name: camel-env-msg
      ports:
      - containerPort: 8080
        name: http
        protocol: TCP
```

The resource now has the desired variable in its definition. Let's test it on minikube.

In the same terminal, configure the Docker variables like this:

```
camel-env-msg $ eval $(minikube -p minikube docker-env)
```

Create a new namespace for this test:

```
$ kubectl create namespace third-deploy
```

Set your client context to the new namespace:

```
$ kubectl config set-context --current --namespace=third-deploy
```

Then you can deploy the application like this:

```
camel-env-msg $ mvn clean package \
-Dquarkus.kubernetes.deployment-target=minikube \
-Dquarkus.kubernetes.deploy=true
```

Once the deployment is done, get the URL information using

```
$ minikube service list
```

In my case, the result was Figure 6-13.

```
~ $ minikube service list
|---------------|---------------|---------------|------------------------------|
|   NAMESPACE   |     NAME      |  TARGET PORT  |             URL              |
|---------------|---------------|---------------|------------------------------|
| default       | kubernetes    | No node port  |                              |
| kube-system   | kube-dns      | No node port  |                              |
| third-deploy  | camel-env-msg | http/8080     | http://192.168.64.14:30410   |
|---------------|---------------|---------------|------------------------------|
```

Figure 6-13. *Service list result*

In my environment, the test call is like this:

```
$ curl http://192.168.64.10:30410/helloEnv
```

The expected response is "Message from ENV var" as set in the resource definition, but once the image is built, you can make changes to the deployment definition and change how the application behaves.

You can change resources in more than one way. For example, you could use kubectl edit deployment ${name} and manually edit the resource using a command line editor, but for this example you can use a more straight-to-the-point approach.

Run the following command to change the deployment:

```
$ kubectl patch deploy camel-env-msg --type='json' -p='[{"op":
"replace","path":"/spec/template/spec/containers/0/env/1/
value", "value":"new patched message"}]'
```

I'm not passing the namespace in the call because the context is already set to the correct namespace. If you changed the context in your client configuration, just add `-n third-deploy` to the command.

Patching the deployment will cause a new deployment to happen. You may see that by checking the events by running this:

```
$ kubectl get events
```

Try another request. You should get a response like Figure 6-14.

```
~ $ curl -w '\n' http://192.168.64.14:30410/helloEnv
new patched message
```

Figure 6-14. *Patched message*

Once you are done testing, you may delete the namespace:

```
$ kubectl delete namespace third-deploy
```

This example's objective is to show you that it is possible to use environment variables to configure your Quarkus application and how easy it is to use the extensions to create a deployment resource with those definitions.

Here you set the variable in the resource definition, but Kubernetes is more flexible than that. You could use configMaps or secrets as a value for the variable, although this does not change how the application gets to access the variable.

ConfigMaps and Secrets

ConfigMaps and Secrets are Kubernetes resources that allow users to separate images from the configuration. They are a key-value file that can host simple string values to complete files. The difference between the two is that Secrets are normally used to save more sensitive data, as Secrets, by default, are stored as unencrypted base64-encoded strings. Let's see how to use these resources with Quarkus and Camel.

For this example, you are going to use the camel-cm-secret project. Open it in your IDE and let's analyze this project route, shown in Listing 6-8.

Listing 6-8. ConfigMapSecretRoute.java File

```
public class ConfigMapSecretRoute extends RouteBuilder {

@Override
public void configure() throws Exception {

rest("/ConfigMapSecret")
.get()
.route()
.routeId("cm-secret")
.log("Request Received")
.choice()
.when(header("password").isEqualTo(constant("{{password}}" )))
   .setBody(constant("{{application.message}}"))
   .log("Authorized")
.otherwise()
   .setHeader(Exchange.HTTP_RESPONSE_CODE, constant(403))
   .log("Not Authorized")
.endRest();

  }
}
```

You are going to use this REST route to simulate an authentication process. It will check if the "password" header is equal to a given value and if it is, a message will be sent to the client. If the header is not present or not equal to the expected value, a 403 response code will be returned to the client.

Using predicates is definitely not something new, but the new trick is in this project application.properties file, shown in Listing 6-9.

Listing 6-9. Camel-cm-secret application.properties File

```
# Route properties
%dev.application.message=Authorized
%dev.password=test

# Kubernetes configuration
quarkus.container-image.group=apress

## Secret mount
quarkus.kubernetes.mounts.my-volume.path=/work/config/
application.properties
quarkus.kubernetes.mounts.my-volume.sub-path=application.
properties
quarkus.kubernetes.secret-volumes.my-volume.secret-name=app-
secret

## ConfigMap Environment Variable
quarkus.kubernetes.env.mapping.application-message.from-
configmap=app-config
quarkus.kubernetes.env.mapping.application-message.with-
key=app.msg
```

Starting with the route properties, you have something new here. Quarkus allows you to use the same `application.properties` files to declare properties for different profiles. Each profile is used for specific environments such as dev, test, and prod. In this example, you are using a dev profile, which is going to be used when you run the code using the plugin `quarkus:dev`, but is not used when running the jar.

In the secret mount part, you are going to mount a secret as a properties file under the `/work/config` directory and load it as the `application.properties`. To facilitate the understanding, you could read the properties key like this:

```
quarkus.kubernetes.mounts.[volume name].path
quarkus.kubernetes.mounts.[volume name].sub-path
quarkus.kubernetes.secret-volumes.[volume name].secret-name
```

You already saw how to use environment variables with Quarkus, but here you are using them in a different way. Instead of setting the value directly, you are going to get the value from a `configMap` using a property key. You could read the keys like this:

```
quarkus.kubernetes.env.mapping.[ENV VAR].from-configmap
quarkus.kubernetes.env.mapping.[ENV VAR].with-key
```

Let's see how the deployment definition will look. Pack the application like this:

```
camel-cm-secret $ mvn clean package \
-Dquarkus.kubernetes.deployment-target=minikube
```

Look at the `target/kubenetes/minikube.yaml` file in Listing 6-10.

Listing 6-10. Camel-cm-secret minikube.yaml Deployment

```
apiVersion: apps/v1
kind: Deployment
metadata:
  annotations:
  labels:
    app.kubernetes.io/name: camel-cm-secret
    app.kubernetes.io/version: 1.0.0
  name: camel-cm-secret
spec:
  replicas: 1
  selector:
    matchLabels:
      app.kubernetes.io/name: camel-cm-secret
      app.kubernetes.io/version: 1.0.0
  template:
    metadata:
      annotations:
      labels:
        app.kubernetes.io/name: camel-cm-secret
        app.kubernetes.io/version: 1.0.0
    spec:
      containers:
      - env:
        - name: KUBERNETES_NAMESPACE
          valueFrom:
            fieldRef:
              fieldPath: metadata.namespace
        - name: APPLICATION_MESSAGE
```

```
        valueFrom:
          configMapKeyRef:
            key: app.msg
            name: app-config
      image: apress/camel-cm-secret:1.0.0
      imagePullPolicy: IfNotPresent
      name: camel-cm-secret
      ports:
      - containerPort: 8080
        name: http
        protocol: TCP
      volumeMounts:
      - mountPath: /work/config/application.properties
        name: my-volume
        readOnly: false
        subPath: application.properties
    volumes:
    - name: my-volume
      secret:
        defaultMode: 384
        optional: false
        secretName: app-secret
```

You have the environment variable APPLICATION_MESSAGE using a configMap reference for its value and a volume to mount the Secret. Now you can start to set up the environment for the test.

First, you need to create a new namespace to test this application. In a terminal window, run the following command:

```
$ kubectl create namespace forth-deploy
```

Set the client context to the newly created namespace:

```
$ kubectl config set-context --current --namespace=forth-deploy
```

The application will need a configMap and a Secret configured in the namespace. Let's provide them, starting with the Secret:

```
$ echo "password=admin" >> application.properties

$ kubectl create secret generic app-secret \
--from-file=application.properties

$ rm application.properties
```

And then create the configMap like this:

```
$ kubectl create cm app-config \
--from-literal=app.msg="Message from CM"
```

To deploy the application, navigate to the camel-cm-secret directory. This time you are going to set which node-port you are going to use by setting the quarkus.kubernetes.node-port property:

```
camel-cm-secret $ eval $(minikube -p minikube docker-env)
camel-cm-secret $ mvn clean package \
-Dquarkus.kubernetes.deployment-target=minikube \
-Dquarkus.kubernetes.deploy=true \
-Dquarkus.kubernetes.node-port=30241
```

By setting the node-port you now have a predictable address to send requests to. You can test in your machine using the following command:

```
$ curl http://$(minikube ip):30241/ConfigMapSecret \
-H "password: admin"
```

Expect to receive a message equal to Figure 6-15.

```
~ $ curl http://$(minikube ip):30241/ConfigMapSecret \
> -H "password: admin" -w '\n'
Message from CM
```

Figure 6-15. *ConfigMapSecret response*

You can keep testing by sending wrong passwords or changing the Secret or the `configMap` but remember that changes to these resources won't trigger new deployments. If you have changed those resources, you can "bounce" the application pod like this:

```
$ kubectl delete pod ${pod-name}
```

Replace the variable ${pod-name} by the pod name. You can get the name using this command:

```
$ kubectl get pods
```

When you delete a pod, a controller will create a new pod to replace the deleted one, maintaining the deployment's defined desired state. Volumes and environment variable values are evaluated when pods are being deployed.

Once you are finished with your testing, delete the namespace:

```
$ kubectl delete namespace forth-deploy
```

Health Check and Probes

Health checks are a big deal for monitoring applications in production. You need to know if applications are up and running and do the right measures if they are not. When you are dealing with containerized applications running in Kubernetes this functionally becomes mandatory. Let's see why.

The beauty of using Kubernetes is the amount of automation it performs for us to keep our applications running but also scalable. To do so, Kubernetes needs to know how to evaluate if an application is responsive and ready to receive requests. Examine Figure 6-16.

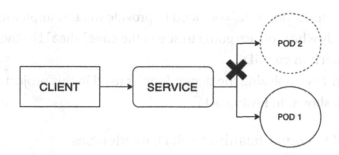

Figure 6-16. *Service load balancing*

Client applications inside the cluster will usually access other pods through name using `services`. Although `services` are only an abstraction for how Kubernetes handles service discovery and load balancing, what is important for you to know is that they have the ability to identify if an endpoint (pod) is ready to receive a request. In Figure 6-16, the second pod could be a new one because the deployment got scaled or it could be the second replica getting restarted because it entered in a failed state. In both situations the application is not ready to receive a request, so the service layer will redirect all the requests to the first pod.

In order to identify the application state, Kubernetes defines test routines called probes. There are three: Readiness, Liveness, and Startup.

`Readiness` and `Startup` are probes made to identify if the application is ready to receive connections. The Startup probe is more ideal for legacy applications that might require an additional startup time on their first initialization. You won't be dealing with the Startup probe in this book because you are creating modern applications that start really fast.

`Liveness` is a test to check if the application is responsive. This way you can identify if a running application is not hung in a deadlock and restart it if it is.

You can use HTTP calls, TPC port checks, or execute a command in the container to perform the tests. There are different parameters regarding error tolerance, delays between attempts, timeouts, and so on that make these diagnostics flexible enough to handle different types of applications. You will see some possibilities when studying the example.

On the application side, you need to provide the test implementations. This is exactly what you are going to see in the camel-health-check project. Open it in your IDE.

Let's start by analyzing the dependencies used in this project. Open the pom.xml file shown in Listing 6-11.

Listing 6-11. camel-health-check Dependencies

```
...
<dependencies>
<dependency>
<groupId>org.apache.camel.quarkus</groupId>
<artifactId>camel-quarkus-rest</artifactId>
</dependency>
<dependency>
<groupId>io.quarkus</groupId>
<artifactId>quarkus-container-image-jib</artifactId>
</dependency>
<dependency>
<groupId>io.quarkus</groupId>
<artifactId>quarkus-minikube</artifactId>
</dependency>
<dependency>
<groupId>io.quarkus</groupId>
<artifactId>quarkus-smallrye-health</artifactId>
</dependency>
</dependencies>
...
```

Camel provides mechanisms to create health checks, but what you are going to use is another SmallRye project that implements the MicroProfile Health specification, SmallRye Health. You are going to use it because it is very flexible but also integrated with the Kubernetes plugin, so the

Quarkus configuration will be reflected in the generated Deployment document without having to add more configuration.

Take a look at the testing route shown in Listing 6-12.

Listing 6-12. HealthCheckRoute.java File

```java
public class HealthCheckRoute extends RouteBuilder {

    @Override
    public void configure() throws Exception {
      rest("/healthApp")
      .get()
          .route()
          .routeId("health-route")
          .log("Request Received")
          .setBody(constant("{{application.message}}"))
      .endRest();

    }
}
```

This is another "Hello World" type of route, because what you really need to study is not the route, but how you are handling the health checks.

Start by opening the AppReadiness class shown in Listing 6-13.

Listing 6-13. AppReadiness.java File

```java
@Readiness
@Singleton
public class AppReadiness implements HealthCheck {

private static final Logger LOG = Logger.
getLogger(AppReadiness.class);

@Inject
CamelContext context;
```

251

```java
@Override
public HealthCheckResponse call() {

LOG.trace("Testing Readiness");

HealthCheckResponseBuilder builder;

if(context.isStarted()){
  builder = HealthCheckResponse.named("Context UP").up();
}else{
  builder = HealthCheckResponse.named("Context Down").down();
}

 return builder.build();

}
}
```

You start by implementing the HealthCheck interface, which defines a single method, call(). This method is where you identify if the application is ready to receive connections. Since this is a simple REST application, you readiness condition is the Camel context being started. To check the context, you injected the context in the Singleton bean and used the context method isStarted() to do the verification. Based on the method returned, a positive (up()) or negative (down()) HealCheckResponse is given. To make this HealthCheck valid for readiness, you only need to add the annotation @Readiness.

Now let's take a look at how the Liveness test is done. See Listing 6-14.

Listing 6-14. AppLiveness.java File

```java
@Liveness
@Singleton
public class AppLiveness implements HealthCheck {
```

```
private static final Logger LOG = Logger.getLogger(AppLiveness.
class);

@Inject
CamelContext context;

@Override
public HealthCheckResponse call() {

  LOG.trace("Testing Liveness");

  HealthCheckResponseBuilder builder;

  if(!context.isStopped()){
     builder = HealthCheckResponse.named("Camel UP").up();
  }else{
     builder = HealthCheckResponse.namcd("Camel DOWN").down();
  }

  return builder.build();
}
}
```

This health check is very similar to the AppReadiness, but instead of checking if the context is started, you check if the context is not stopped. If the context is stopped, it means that your route is not running, therefore the application needs to be restarted.

To make this health check as your Liveness test, you only need to add the @Liveness annotation to the class.

The Camel context will only be stopped if you program it to be or when the application receives a SIGTERM to gracefully shutdown, but it still serves as an example of how to implement liveness.

You may have noticed that you have trace logs in both health checks. Those logs help you to see how those tests are invoked by Kubelet. Take a look at the `application.properties` file. You are enabling trace logs only for the health checks. See Listing 6-15.

Listing 6-15. Camel-health-check application.properties File

```
# Quarkus properties
quarkus.log.category."com.apress.integration.health".level
=TRACE
quarkus.log.min-level=TRACE

# Route properties
application.message=Hello from HealthApp

# Kubernetes configuration
quarkus.container-image.group=apress
```

Let's generate the Deployment definition. In a terminal, navigate to the `camel-health-check` directory and run the following command:

```
camel-health-check $ mvn clean package \
-Dquarkus.kubernetes.deployment-target=minikube
```

Open the generated file, `target/kubernetes/minikube.yaml`. Let's examine the pod definition inside the Deployment. See Listing 6-16.

Listing 6-16. Deployment Pod Spec

```
...
  template:
    metadata:
      annotations:
      labels:
        app.kubernetes.io/name: camel-health-check
```

```
    app.kubernetes.io/version: 1.0.0
spec:
  containers:
  - env:
    - name: KUBERNETES_NAMESPACE
      valueFrom:
        fieldRef:
          fieldPath: metadata.namespace
    image: apress/camel-health-check:1.0.0
    imagePullPolicy: IfNotPresent
    livenessProbe:
      failureThreshold: 3
      httpGet:
        path: /q/health/live
        port: 8080
        scheme: HTTP
      initialDelaySeconds: 0
      periodSeconds: 30
      successThreshold: 1
      timeoutSeconds: 10
    name: camel-health-check
    ports:
    - containerPort: 8080
      name: http
      protocol: TCP
    readinessProbe:
      failureThreshold: 3
      httpGet:
        path: /q/health/ready
        port: 8080
        scheme: HTTP
```

```
initialDelaySeconds: 0
periodSeconds: 30
successThreshold: 1
timeoutSeconds: 10
```

As you can see, the Readiness and Liveness probes are declared with all the necessary information, using default values for the test parameters. These default values are sufficient for you to test this specific application in minikube. This application is light and fast so having a zero-second delay for the first attempt after the container started is not a problem since the application starts within milliseconds. The tests will be made in a thirty second interval and only after three consecutive failures the probe will be considered as failed. To get back to a successful state only a successful attempt is required.

These parameters are important because you don't want to be super aggressive in how you consider that an application failed. You may have access picks that may degrade the application performance but it may still be running properly, and restarting the application may only aggravate the issue.

What you are trying to do with this configuration is generate the most optimal configuration that allows pods to receive connections as fast as they are ready and identify, as fast you can, when a pod is failing to avoid propagating errors to client applications. The only way to reach this most optimal configuration is by testing the application under different scenarios.

To test this application, open a terminal window and navigate to the camel-health-check/ directory. Start by creating a new namespace for this deployment:

```
camel-health-check $ kubectl create namespace fifth-deploy
```

Set the client context to the new namespace:

```
camel-health-check $ kubectl config set-context
--current     --namespace=fifth-deploy
```

Before running the deployment, set the Docker variables:

```
camel-health-check $ eval $(minikube -p minikube docker-env)
```

Deploy the application:

```
camel-health-check $ mvn clean package \
-Dquarkus.kubernetes.deployment-target=minikube \
-Dquarkus.kubernetes.deploy=true \
-Dquarkus.kubernetes.node-port=30241
```

You can use this command to test the application:

```
$ curl http://$(minikube ip):30241/healthApp
```

Testing is interesting to check if the deployment went fine, but what you are looking to see here is how the health checks are being invoked. To do so, you need to check the logs. You can check them by running this:

```
$ kubectl logs -f deploy/camel-health-check
```

Using -f will allow you to continuously follow the logs as they appear. Once you get some entries, like Listing 6-17, you may stop it using Control+ C.

Listing 6-17. Camel-health-check Logs Output

```
2021-06-16 23:45:20,975 INFO  [io.quarkus] (main) camel-health-
check 1.0.0 on JVM (powered by Quarkus 1.13.0.Final) started in
3.051s. Listening on: http://0.0.0.0:8080
2021-06-16 23:45:20,976 INFO  [io.quarkus] (main) Profile prod
activated.
```

```
2021-06-16 23:45:20,977 INFO  [io.quarkus] (main) Installed
features: [camel-attachments, camel-core, camel-platform-http,
camel-rest, camel-support-common, cdi, kubernetes, mutiny,
smallrye-context-propagation, smallrye-health, vertx, vertx-web]
2021-06-16 23:45:43,078 TRACE [com.apr.int.hea.AppReadiness]
(vert.x-worker-thread-0) Testing Readiness
2021-06-16 23:45:46,522 TRACE [com.apr.int.hea.AppLiveness]
(vert.x-worker-thread-1) Testing Liveness
2021-06-16 23:46:12,661 TRACE [com.apr.int.hea.AppReadiness]
(vert.x-worker-thread-2) Testing Readiness
2021-06-16 23:46:16,520 TRACE [com.apr.int.hea.AppLiveness]
(vert.x-worker-thread-3) Testing Liveness
```

You can see that after the application starts properly, every thirty seconds a new test for readiness and liveness is made on the application.

Another test that can be made is to open two terminal windows side by side. In one terminal, run this command to watch the available pods:

```
$ kubectl get pods -w
```

In the second terminal, run the following command to scale the deployment by adding one replica:

```
$ kubectl scale deploy/camel-health-check --replicas=2
```

You will see that it will take some time for the new pod to move from Ready 0/1 to 1/1, as in Figure 6-17. This is the time the container takes to pass the Readiness test.

```
~ $ kubectl get pods -w
NAME                                READY  STATUS            RESTARTS  AGE
camel-health-check-69dff7bd76-hx8z6  1/1   Running           0         49s
camel-health-check-69dff7bd76-6vtn8  0/1   Pending           0         0s
camel-health-check-69dff7bd76-6vtn8  0/1   Pending           0         0s
camel-health-check-69dff7bd76-6vtn8  0/1   ContainerCreating 0                 0s
camel-health-check-69dff7bd76-6vtn8  0/1   Running           0                 4s
camel-health-check-69dff7bd76-6vtn8  1/1   Running           0                 17s
```

Figure 6-17. Pod scaling

Request and Limits

I talked about the Scheduler component, which is responsible for allocating pods to the appropriate nodes. But what does "appropriate" mean in this context? Besides specific parameters such as node labeling and node features, it means to have the necessary amount of resources to accommodate the pods. Since the scheduler cannot guess what the application needs, you have to set default values for the namespace you have, or you can set those values in the deployment definition. Requests and Limits are ways to tell Kubernetes how much resources you believe the application should consume.

Here you are going to focus on two different resources, CPU and RAM. There are other resources to restrict usage, but CPU and RAM are the most commonly used to determine pod placement. Analyze Figure 6-18 to see how pod placement works.

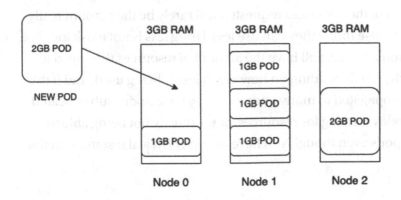

Figure 6-18. The pod placement process

In this example, you have a three-node cluster with 3GB of RAM each for pod allocation. You have a new pod generated for this cluster and only Node 0 has enough resources to host this 2GB pod.

Although not demonstrated in the figure, the same goes for CPU. Each node has its amount of available CPU capacity for pod allocation. If a new pod has its requirements specified, the scheduler will try to find a node that matches the amount of CPU and RAM requested by the pod.

Requests are the amount of resources that a pod is expected to consume from a node and the basic measure for node capacity.

When a pod definition doesn't have requests declared, the scheduler will place it in any node that has resources still available, but the available resources may not be enough for this new pod, causing out-of-memory (OOM) errors or impacting the application performance if the node doesn't have enough CPU available.

You can define requests and limits per container and per pod. Here you are focusing on pod declaration because you are going to use it in the example.

Application resource consumption is usually not linear. It will depend on what is being processed or the amount of access it has in a given time, so the amount of the resources requested will rarely be the amount really used. They can use more; they can use less. Using less is not a risk for the applications, as they will have the amount of resources they need to work properly, but depending on how much less is being used, and if this behavior is propagated to many pods, you may have nodes sub allocated and other nodes starving for resources, or eventually not being able to deploy new pods even though you have enough physical resources in the cluster.

Limits are used to give applications the flexibility to use more resources when eventually needed, but also to put a hard ceiling on how much can be consumed. If an application tries to use more memory than its limit, Kubelet will kill the application, causing it to restart to fix the problem.

CPU usage is different. Since the metric for CPU is time allocation, the application won't be able to use more CPU than its limit.

To materialize these concepts, let's enable some features in your running minikube. First, you need to add a component to monitor resource usage by the pods. Run the following command to install the metrics server in minikube:

```
$ minikube addons enable metrics-server
```

Once the add-on is installed, you can use minikube's dashboard to visualize metrics. Run the following command to open it on your browser:

```
$ minikube dashboard
```

This command will lead you to the dashboard home page, shown in Figure 6-19.

Figure 6-19. *minikube dashboard*

This dashboard allows you to visualize, create, edit, and delete the Kubernetes resources in minikube. You have been using the command line because it makes the example steps more reproducible, but if you are a GUI fan, the dashboard can be a good alternative for you.

What you want to see in this dashboard is how much resources the application you used in the latest section is consuming. To do so, follow these steps:

- On the top of the screen in the dropdown box. Select the namespace `fifth-deploy`.

- On the left side panel, click Pods.

There you have it. You should see something similar to Figure 6-20.

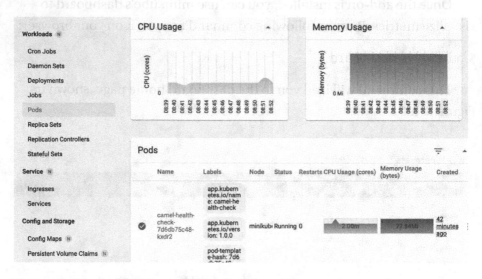

Figure 6-20. *minikube metrics dashboard*

As you can see, one of the pods is consuming 2 millicores of CPU and something around 73 mebibyte of memory.

A millicore is a measure to declare CPU time allocation. Every core or virtual core in a machine is given a total of 1000 millicores points, independent of the type of CPU. These points are used to determine processing prioritization, so the more points the container has, the more time it will have to consume CPU. In my case, my minikube instance is using the default value for MacOS, 2 CPUS, which represents 2000 millicores or 2 cores.

A mebibyte is just a different way to represent memory allocation, where 1 MiB = 2^{20} bytes or 1,048,576 bytes. Meanwhile 1MB is 10^{6} or 1,000,000 bytes. If you want to know how much 73Mi means in MB, just multiply the bytes for 1.04858, which is 76.546MB.

Now that you know how much this application consumes from the start, let's make some adjustments to it in the deployment configuration.

Open the `camel-health-check` project in your IDE. Open `application.properties` and add the following lines to it:

```
#Requests
quarkus.kubernetes.resources.requests.memory=44Mi
quarkus.kubernetes.resources.requests.cpu=10m
#Limits
quarkus.kubernetes.resources.limits.memory=50Mi
quarkus.kubernetes.resources.limits.cpu=100m
```

Let's generate the deployment resource:

```
camel-health-check $ mvn clean package \
-Dquarkus.kubernetes.deployment-target=minikube
```

Look at the template in the deployment definition, shown in Listing 6-18.

Listing 6-18. Template Definition with Request and Limits

```
...
  template:
    metadata:
      annotations:
      labels:
        app.kubernetes.io/name: camel-health-check
        app.kubernetes.io/version: 1.0.0
    spec:
      containers:
      - env:
        - name: KUBERNETES_NAMESPACE
          valueFrom:
            fieldRef:
              fieldPath: metadata.namespace
        image: apress/camel-health-check:1.0.0
        imagePullPolicy: IfNotPresent
        livenessProbe:
          failureThreshold: 3
          httpGet:
            path: /q/health/live
            port: 8080
            scheme: HTTP
          initialDelaySeconds: 0
          periodSeconds: 30
          successThreshold: 1
          timeoutSeconds: 10
        name: camel-health-check
```

```
ports:
- containerPort: 8080
  name: http
  protocol: TCP
readinessProbe:
  failureThreshold: 3
  httpGet:
    path: /q/health/ready
    port: 8080
    scheme: HTTP
  initialDelaySeconds: 0
  periodSeconds: 30
  successThreshold: 1
  timeoutSeconds: 10
resources:
  limits:
    cpu: 100m
    memory: 50Mi
  requests:
    cpu: 10m
    memory: 44Mi
```

The definitions are added to the pod, since with this plugin you will only have a single container per deployment.

You know that 44Mi is less than what is used by the application, but what would happen to the deployment under this condition? Let's check by testing.

First, delete the older namespace:

```
$ kubectl delete namespace fifth-deploy
```

Now let's create a new namespace for this test, set the context for the client, set the Docker variables, and deploy the application.

Navigate to the camel-health-check directory and run the following commands:

```
camel-health-check $ kubectl create namespace sixth-deploy
camel-health-check $ kubectl config set-context
--current       --namespace=sixth-deploy

camel-health-check $ eval $(minikube -p minikube docker-env)

camel-health-check $ mvn clean package \
-Dquarkus.kubernetes.deployment-target=minikube \
-Dquarkus.kubernetes.deploy=true \
-Dquarkus.kubernetes.node-port=30241
```

Once the deployment is finished, monitor the namespace pods using this command:

```
$ kubectl get pod -w
```

You will see that the deployment will never properly finish because you are not giving the application the required amount of memory to start up, and when the application tries to consume more memory than its limit, the Kubelet will act on it and kill it, as you can see in Figure 6-21.

```
NAME                                    READY   STATUS            RESTARTS   AGE
camel-health-check-7c45bbd595-515tm     0/1     OOMKilled         1          54s
camel-health-check-7c45bbd595-515tm     0/1     CrashLoopBackOff  1          65s
camel-health-check-7c45bbd595-515tm     0/1     Running           2          66s
camel-health-check-7c45bbd595-515tm     0/1     CrashLoopBackOff  2          68s
camel-health-check-7c45bbd595-515tm     0/1     Running           3          96s
camel-health-check-7c45bbd595-515tm     0/1     OOMKilled         3          116s
camel-health-check-7c45bbd595-515tm     0/1     CrashLoopBackOff  3          2m7s
```

Figure 6-21. *OOMKilled*

The probes, requests, and limits also require thorough tests to configure the best balance between expected resource consumption and resource consumption under access pick. Have in mind that when using containers, you ideally scale horizontally, which means creating more pods, instead of just adding more resources to a single pod. I said "ideally" because you will find situations where containers cannot scale and in these situations only vertical scaling will be possible.

You are done with tests using minikube. At this point, you can stop it and delete your instance if you like:

```
$ minikube stop
$ minikube delete
```

Summary

This was the last chapter in this book, and it was an audacious one. Kubernetes is just too much ground to cover, but I tried to keep the conversation more related to applications than the challenge of managing a Kubernetes cluster. You learned the following in this chapter:

- What Kubernetes is and the benefits of using it

- How to experiment with Kubernetes from a development perspective using minikube

- How to deploy Quarkus applications into Kubernetes using Quarkus extensions

- What you need to know about application configuration to deploy applications into Kubernetes

The idea of this book is to create a solid learning path for developers and architects who have integration needs and will have to solve them using containers and Kubernetes. You saw from the very basics of how to run Camel applications in your machine, to generating an image and deploying it to Kubernetes, with practical examples that you will be able to reference in the future.

I hope that you feel enabled to create your own integrations using modern technologies and architectural designs. I'll see you in a future tech discussion.

Index

Printed in the United States
by Baker & Taylor Publisher Services

Printed in the United States
by Baker & Taylor Publisher Services